Best bakes

Seven C3

Produced by Seven Publishing Ltd on behalf of
WW International, Inc. Published March 2021.

Seven Publishing Ltd
3-7 Herbal Hill
London EC1R 5EJ
seven.co.uk

10 9 8 7 6 5 4 3 2 1

ISBN: 978-1-8381473-2-7

WW PUBLISHING TEAM
Samantha Rees, Harriet Joy,
Jessica O'Shea

FOR SEVEN PUBLISHING LTD
EDITORIAL
Content lead: Helena Lang
Editor: Christine Faughlin
Sub-editor: Tom Shepherd

FOOD
Food director: Sarah Akhurst
Food editor: Tamsin Burnett-Hall
Recipes: Sarah Akhurst, Linzi Brechin,
Nadine Brown, Gabriella English, Catherine
Hill, Anita Janusic, Ella Tarn, Hannah Yeadon

DESIGN & PHOTOGRAPHY
Art director: Liz Baird
Photographers: Ant Duncan, Jonathan
Kennedy, Kris Kirkham, Adrian Lawrence,
Stuart Ovenden, Vinnie Whiteman
Food stylists: Sarah Cook, Matthew Ford,
Catherine Hill, Emily Kydd, Bianca Nice,
Vicki Smallwood, Ella Tarn
Prop stylists: Linda Berlin, Tamzin
Ferdinando, Claire Morgan, Rob Merrett,
Luis Peral, Davina Perkins, Zoe Regoczy,
Tonya Shuttleworth, Louie Waller,
Polly Webb-Wilson
Additional photography: WW Asset Bank

ACCOUNT MANAGEMENT
Senior account manager: Gina Cavaciuti
Group publishing & client director:
Kirsten Price

PRODUCTION
Print lead: Liz Knipe
Colour reproduction by F1 Colour
Printed in the UK by Bell & Bain Ltd

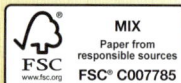

FSC
MIX
Paper from
responsible sources
www.fsc.org
FSC® C007785

Contents

Welcome

There are few things in life more pleasurable than the aroma of freshly baked bread, cakes or biscuits filling your home. And in uncertain times, there's something reassuring, even mindful, about assembling your ingredients, mixing bowls and tins and just focusing on the job at hand. That you end up with a beautiful homemade treat to enjoy or give to nearby friends and family is, so to speak, the icing on the cake. Whether you're an experienced cook or new to baking, prefer sweet treats or savoury bakes, the recipes in this book will provide plenty of inspiration. It's an exciting collection of our best-ever bakes – the cakes, pastries, biscuits and puds that members in the UK and around the world really love to make – and eat. Happy baking!

Be a better baker...

Whether you're new to baking or a seasoned pro, our tips, tricks and advice will help you to turn out brilliant bakes every time.

1 Add some crunch
When making shortbread, replace 2 tablespoonfuls of flour with the same amount of ground rice, semolina or polenta to add some crunch. Remember to adjust the SmartPoints.

2 Swap your sugar
Swap light brown soft sugar for caster sugar to give your bakes a fuller flavour, richer colour and fudgier, chewier texture.

3 Pipe down
When filling a piping bag, place it in an empty glass or measuring jug, nozzle down, then fold the edges over the rim. This leaves both hands free for easier, less-messy filling.

4 Line up
The easiest way to line a loaf tin is to cut two long strips of baking paper then lay them in the tin to form a cross. For a quick liner for a traybake, there's no need to cut and fold to shape, simply tear off a sheet of baking paper and crumple it into a ball, then open it out and press into the corners of the tin.

5 Toasted nuts

If you're using nuts in a cake or bake, bring out their full flavour by toasting them lightly first in the oven.

6 Dip, dunk, drizzle

Put melted chocolate for dipping in a small bowl or even in a mug, so that you have a good depth for easy dunking. Coat no more than half of a biscuit or slice; you get the same flavour for fewer SmartPoints. Or drizzle on instead, to use even less chocolate.

7 Measure up

More than any other form of cooking, baking calls for precision to get good results. Use measuring spoons and digital scales for accuracy. You can even measure liquids by weight (1ml = 1g), rather than in a measuring jug.

8 Better bread

Don't over-prove shaped bread dough before baking; it should just feel pillowy when you press it lightly.

9 Just the one

Make biscuits, muffins, cupcakes or other individually portioned bakes if it helps you to be more conscious of how much you're eating and staying on track.

10 Even distribution

To help prevent dried fruit from sinking to the bottom of a cake, use a little of the measured flour to toss with the dried fruit before you make the cake batter.

11 Stir and scrape

Use a flexible silicone spatula to get every last scrap of cake batter out of the bowl. It's great for mixing and folding ingredients in too.

12 Size matters

Use an ice cream scoop to help fill muffin or cupcake cases evenly.

13 Keep your cool

Be patient and let cakes cool completely before assembling or icing them.

14 Light and airy

Cream spread and sugar for at least 3 minutes to beat in lots of air.

15 Finishing touch

Decorate your bakes with ZeroPoint fresh fruit, mint leaves, citrus zest or edible flowers.

About our recipes

Our cookbooks are packed with healthy recipes you'll want to make time and time again.

Our philosophy is simple: to offer recipes that are nutritious as well as delicious. Our recipes are designed to encourage a healthier pattern of eating with lots of ZeroPoint foods and lower SmartPoints value ingredients to make the most of your Budget. Here's how to better understand our recipes and the ingredients that go into them.

Ingredients

EGGS We use medium eggs, unless otherwise stated. Pregnant women, the elderly and children should avoid recipes with eggs which are raw or not fully cooked if not produced under the British Lion code of practice.

FRUIT AND VEGETABLES Recipes use medium-size fruit and veg, unless otherwise stated.

LOW-FAT SPREAD When a recipe uses a low-fat spread, we mean a spread with a fat content of no more than 39 per cent.

REDUCED-FAT SOFT CHEESE Where a recipe uses medium-fat soft cheese, we mean a cheese with 30 per cent less fat than its full-fat equivalent; where a recipe uses low-fat soft cheese, we mean a soft cheese with 5 per cent fat.

Prep and cook instructions

PREP AND COOK TIMES These are approximate and meant to be guidelines only. Prep time includes all steps up to and following the main cooking time(s). Stated cook times may vary according to your oven.

MICROWAVES If we've used a microwave, the timings are for an 850-watt microwave oven.

Dietary requirements

VEGETARIAN RECIPES Recipes displaying a vegetarian symbol include non-meat ingredients, but may also contain processed products that aren't always vegetarian, such as pesto. If you're a vegetarian, ensure you use vegetarian varieties and check the ingredients labels. Where we reference vegetarian Italian-style hard cheese in vegetarian recipes, we mean a cheese that's similar to Parmesan (which is not vegetarian) but is suitable for vegetarians. For more info and guidance, visit www.vegsoc.org

VEGAN RECIPES Recipes with a vegan symbol include no products made from or with the aid of

'Our recipes are designed to encourage a healthier pattern of eating'

animals or animal products. If you are vegan, ensure you use vegan varieties of processed ingredients (such as pesto) and check product labels to ensure ingredients have never been tested on animals. For more info and guidance, visit www.vegansociety.com

GLUTEN-FREE RECIPES Recipes that are labelled as gluten free include ingredients that naturally do not contain gluten, but they may also contain processed products, such as sauces, stock cubes and spice mixes. If so,

ensure that those products do not include any gluten-containing ingredients (wheat, barley or rye) – these will be highlighted in the ingredients list on the product label. Manufacturers may also indicate if there's a chance their product has been contaminated with gluten during manufacturing. For more information and guidance on gluten-free products, visit www.coeliac.org.uk

NUT-FREE RECIPES Recipes displaying a nut free symbol include ingredients that do not contain nuts and/or certain seeds, but may include ingredients produced in facilities that also handle nut products. If you have a nut allergy, check ingredients labels for more information.

DAIRY-FREE RECIPES Recipes displaying a dairy free symbol include ingredients that naturally do not contain dairy, but may include ingredients produced in facilities that also handle dairy products. If you have a dairy allergy, check ingredients labels for more information.

SmartPoints calculations

SmartPoints values for all of the recipes in this book are calculated using the values for generic foods, not brands (except where stated). Tracking using branded items may affect the recorded SmartPoints.

WHEN YOU SEE THESE SYMBOLS:

0 **0** **0**

Tells you the SmartPoints value per serving for each plan
Note: Recipes conform to the icon designations, but tip and serving suggestions may not.

Indicates a recipe is gluten free

Indicates a recipe is vegetarian

Indicates a recipe is vegan

Indicates a recipe is nut free

Indicates a recipe is dairy free

Small bakes & biscuits

Fifteens

makes 24   prep time 20 minutes + chilling

(4) (4) (4) 92 kcal
per 'fifteen'

This Northern Irish fridge cake recipe is easy to make and keeps well. The name comes from the number of biscuits, marshmallows and cherries used in it!

15 low-fat digestive biscuits

15 regular marshmallows, cut into small pieces

15 glacé cherries, quartered

170g condensed milk

60g desiccated coconut

1   Put the biscuits in a food bag and seal. Use a rolling pin to crush them into very small pieces. Tip into a large mixing bowl along with the marshmallows and cherries. Pour over the condensed milk and mix the ingredients until well combined and sticky.

2   Sprinkle half the coconut over a large piece of clingfilm, spreading it out evenly. Tip the mixture onto the coconut and form into a long log about 35cm in length, using the clingfilm to help shape it. Sprinkle more of the coconut over the top and using another piece of clingfilm on top, wrap it tightly. Make sure the log is completely covered in coconut, then twist the ends together to seal.

3   Transfer to the fridge and leave for 4-6 hours or until completely chilled and set. Cut into 24 slices and serve.

•   The fifteens keep in an airtight container in the fridge for up to 1 week. Or, freeze them, sliced and individually wrapped, for up to 1 month.

Cook's tip

This is a great recipe for batch cooking as the finished fifteens keep so well. Simply double the ingredients and form 2 logs in Step 2.

Cinnamon apple madeleines

makes 12   prep time 20 minutes + cooling and chilling   cook time 20 minutes

2 **2** **2** 67 kcal
per madeleine

Tender little cakes that use apple purée to reduce the amount of added sugar. They're a great companion to coffee mornings, and leftovers can be frozen.

1 small apple, peeled, cored and roughly chopped

½ teaspoon vanilla extract

65g low-fat spread

50g plain flour, plus 10g for dusting

1 teaspoon ground cinnamon

½ teaspoon baking powder

1 large egg

3 tablespoons caster sugar

½ teaspoon icing sugar

YOU WILL ALSO NEED

12-hole madeleine tin

1 Put the apple in a heavy-based pan with 50ml water and the vanilla extract. Cover and cook over a low heat for 6-8 minutes until tender. Purée the apple using a stick blender or mini food processor.

2 Melt the spread in a small pan over a low heat. Brush a 12-hole madeleine tin with a little of the melted spread, being sure to get into all the ridges. Dust with the extra flour and shake off any excess. Chill the tin in the fridge while you make the batter.

3 Sift together the remaining flour, cinnamon and baking powder in a small bowl. In a separate bowl, beat the egg using a hand-held electric whisk until thick. Add the caster sugar and continue to beat for about 3 minutes. Add the flour to the egg mixture and gently stir together. Fold in the apple purée and the remaining melted spread, then chill for 30 minutes.

4 Preheat the oven to 190°C, fan 170°C, gas mark 5. Spoon the chilled batter into the prepared madeleine tin, filling the moulds almost to the top, then bake for 11-12 minutes. Carefully remove the madeleines from the tin and put on a wire rack to cool, then dust with the icing sugar to serve.

Cook's tip
If you don't have a madeleine tin, you can bake these in a 12-hole muffin tin instead.

Strawberry 'meringue' drops

makes 40   prep time 15 minutes + cooling   cook time 2 hours

1 **1** **1** 9 kcal per 'meringue' drop

Aquafaba – the liquid left over from a drained can of chickpeas – makes for an excellent vegan alternative to egg whites in these sweet bites.

130ml aquafaba (the drained water from a 400g tin of chickpeas)

½ teaspoon cream of tartar

80g caster sugar

7g pack freeze-dried strawberry pieces or slices

Cook's tip
Try crushing a few 'meringue' drops over vegan yogurt or chopped fresh fruit for a delicious dessert – just remember to adjust the SmartPoints.

1 Preheat the oven to 110°C, fan 90°C, gas mark ¼. Line 2 large baking sheets with baking paper.

2 Put the aquafaba and cream of tartar in a large bowl. Use a hand-held electric whisk on the mixture for 10-12 minutes, until stiff peaks form, then gradually beat in the sugar until smooth and combined.

3 In a mini food processor, pulse the freeze-dried strawberries until you have a finely ground powder. Reserve about ½ teaspoon to sprinkle over the tops, then gently fold the rest into the meringue.

4 Spoon the mixture into a disposable piping bag fitted with a large round nozzle. Pipe 3-4cm circles onto the prepared trays – you'll have enough mixture to make around 40 'meringues'. Bake for 2 hours, until they feel dry to the touch.

5 Turn the oven off, leaving the baking sheets inside so that the 'meringues' dry out for 30 minutes to 1 hour as the oven cools. Sprinkle over the reserved dried strawberry powder before serving.

● The strawberry 'meringue' drops will keep in an airtight container for up to 3 days.

Raspberry friands

makes 10   **prep time 15 minutes + cooling**   **cook time 25 minutes**

(5) (5) (5)   **134 kcal per friand**

Friands are small, almond-based cakes that are popular in Australia and New Zealand. The batter uses just the whites of the eggs, which helps to keep them light and airy.

Calorie controlled cooking spray

85g low-fat spread

100g icing sugar, plus an extra 1 teaspoon for dusting

75g ground almonds

25g plain flour

3 egg whites

125g raspberries

1 Preheat the oven to 200°C, fan 180°C, gas mark 6. Mist 10 holes of a 12-hole friand or muffin tin with cooking spray.

2 Melt the spread in a pan over a low heat, then set aside. Put the icing sugar, ground almonds and flour into a large mixing bowl.

3 In a separate bowl, whisk the egg whites until foamy, but not stiff. Make a well in the centre of the dry ingredients and fold in the egg whites and melted spread, until you have a smooth batter.

4 Divide the batter between 10 of the muffin holes and top each friand with 3 raspberries. Bake for 20-25 minutes, or until golden and a skewer inserted into the centre of a friand comes out clean.

5 Remove from the oven and leave to cool for 10 minutes, then turn out of the tin and leave to cool completely on a wire rack. Serve dusted with the extra icing sugar.

• The friands are best eaten on the day of baking, but they can be frozen for up to 1 month.

Cook's tip

Change it up by stirring the finely grated zest of 1 lemon into the batter at the end of Step 3. Then top each friand with 5 small blueberries instead of the raspberries in Step 4. The SmartPoints will stay the same.

Blackberry meringues with compote

makes 10   prep time 25 minutes + cooling   cook time 1 hour

(6) (6) (6)   130 kcal per meringue

Whether you're out to impress or just want something sweet for yourself, these delightfully chewy, ruby-swirled meringues look and taste great.

325g blackberries

4 egg whites, at room temperature

225g caster sugar

1 teaspoon vanilla extract

500g 0% fat natural Greek yogurt

Cook's tip
If you find that the compote is a little on the tart side, stir through 1 tablespoon agave syrup for no extra SmartPoints.

1   Preheat the oven to 120°C, fan 100°C, gas mark ½. Trace 10 x 6.5cm circles onto a sheet of baking paper and turn so that the tracing marks are on the underside.

2   To make a blackberry purée for the swirl, press 75g of the blackberries through a fine sieve into a bowl. Set aside.

3   Using a hand-held electric whisk, beat the egg whites until they form soft peaks. Add the sugar, one spoon at a time, while still beating, until the sugar has dissolved and the mixture is thick and glossy. Whisk in the vanilla extract.

4   Use a little of the meringue mixture to secure the corners of the baking paper to a baking sheet. Spoon the meringue onto the drawn circles and spread out using a small spatula. Top each meringue with 1 teaspoon of the blackberry purée and swirl it through using a skewer. Reserve any leftover purée to use in the compote. Bake the meringues for 1 hour or until they form a crisp shell. Turn off the oven and leave the meringues to cool in the oven with the door ajar, for several hours or overnight.

5   To make the compote, combine the remaining berries, reserved purée and 1 tablespoon of water in a pan over a low heat. Cook for 2-3 minutes until the berries start to break down and the mixture thickens. Remove from the heat and let cool. Serve each meringue topped with the yogurt and compote.

Mini lemon doughnuts

makes 12   prep time 10 minutes + cooling and setting   cook time 10 minutes

2 **2** **2**   54 kcal
per doughnut

Expect a flavour explosion when you bite into one of these little baked beauties, glazed with a zingy yogurt icing.

Calorie controlled cooking spray

100g plain flour

¼ teaspoon baking powder

¼ teaspoon bicarbonate of soda

Zest of 1 lemon

Pinch of salt

75g 0% fat natural Greek yogurt

25ml skimmed milk

1 egg, beaten

2 tablespoons clear honey

TO DECORATE

1 tablespoon 0% fat natural Greek yogurt

1 tablespoon icing sugar

1 tablespoon lemon juice

Yellow food colouring (optional)

Zest of ½ lemon (optional)

YOU WILL ALSO NEED

12-hole mini doughnut tin

1 Preheat the oven to 200°C, fan 180°C, gas mark 6. Mist a 12-hole mini doughnut tin with cooking spray.

2 Put the flour, baking powder, bicarbonate of soda, lemon zest and salt in a large bowl. Stir to combine and make a well in the centre.

3 In a jug, combine the yogurt, milk, egg and honey. Gradually pour this mixture into the flour, stirring to prevent lumps. Spoon into a piping bag fitted with a plain nozzle and pipe into the prepared tin, filling each hole two-thirds full.

4 Bake for 10 minutes, until risen and golden, then transfer the doughnuts to a cooling rack to cool completely.

5 Make the icing: in a small bowl, stir together the yogurt, icing sugar and lemon juice until smooth. Add a few drops of food colouring, if using.

6 Dip the cooled doughnuts in the icing and return to the wire rack to set – this will take about 10 minutes. Once the icing is firm, sprinkle over the lemon zest, if using.

Cook's tip

Try another citrus flavour; swap the lemon for lime, orange, or even grapefruit! The SmartPoints will remain the same.

Victoria sponge bites

makes 20   **prep time 20 minutes + cooling**   **cook time 20 minutes**

(3) (3) (3)   77 kcal per sponge bite

These miniature versions of everyone's favourite jammy teatime sandwich cake are easy to make and perfect for sharing with family and friends.

Calorie controlled cooking spray

110g low-fat spread

110g caster sugar

2 eggs, lightly beaten

½ teaspoon vanilla extract

110g self-raising flour, sifted

1 teaspoon icing sugar, to dust

FOR THE FILLING

100g 0% fat quark

1 teaspoon icing sugar

½ teaspoon vanilla extract

60g low-calorie strawberry or raspberry jam

YOU WILL ALSO NEED

2 x 12-hole mini muffin tins

Cook's tip
Omit the jam and top the quark filling with lightly crushed fresh raspberries instead. Allow about 2-3 raspberries per bite. The SmartPoints will stay the same.

1 Preheat the oven to 180°C, fan 160°C, gas mark 4. Mist 20 holes of 2 x 12-hole mini muffin tins with cooking spray.

2 Beat together the spread and sugar until smooth. Beat in the egg, a little at a time, along with the vanilla. Fold in the flour until combined.

3 Spoon the mixture into the prepared mini muffin tins and bake for 15-18 minutes, until golden and springy to the touch. Cool in the tin for 10 minutes, then loosen the cakes and remove to a wire rack to cool completely.

4 Meanwhile, make the filling: whisk the quark, icing sugar and vanilla extract together in a small bowl and chill until needed.

5 Slice the cooled sponges in half and sandwich with the vanilla quark mixture and jam. Dust the tops with the icing sugar just before serving.

● The unfilled cakes keep in an airtight container for up to 2 days, though they are best eaten on the day of baking. Or, they can be frozen for up to 1 month.

Savoury breakfast muffins

makes 9   **prep time 20 minutes**   **cook time 35 minutes**

(6) (5) (5)   197 kcal
per muffin

Made with bacon, Cheddar cheese and cherry tomatoes, these savoury bakes are super tasty and ideal for breakfast on the move.

Calorie controlled cooking spray

100g bacon medallions, finely chopped

125g plain flour

125g wholemeal plain flour

2 teaspoons baking powder

½ teaspoon bicarbonate of soda

80g low-fat spread, melted

2 large eggs

200ml semi-skimmed milk

75g half-fat mature Cheddar cheese, grated

100g cherry tomatoes, roughly chopped

Handful fresh chives, finely chopped

1 Preheat the oven to 190°C, fan 170°C, gas mark 5. Line 9 holes of a 12-hole muffin tin with paper cases.

2 Mist a frying pan with cooking spray and fry the bacon over a medium heat for 2-3 minutes, turning occasionally, until golden, then remove from the heat and set aside.

3 In a large bowl, combine the flours, baking powder and bicarbonate of soda, then season.

4 In a separate bowl, beat together the cooled melted spread, eggs, milk and cheese and add to the dry ingredients. Mix well, then stir in the bacon, tomatoes and chives until combined.

5 Divide the mixture between the muffin cases and bake for 25-30 minutes, or until risen and golden.

Cook's tip

Make these vegetarian by replacing the bacon with 125g sliced mushrooms, and 4 trimmed and chopped spring onions.

(5) (5) (5)

Sweet potato muffins

makes 8   prep time 20 minutes + cooling   cook time 35 minutes

6 **5** **5**   169 kcal
per muffin

Fluffy gluten-free morning muffins made with maple syrup, ground almonds and cinnamon for a light, comforting sweetness.

150g sweet potato, peeled and cut into 2cm cubes

2 eggs, lightly beaten

2 tablespoons vegetable oil

4 tablespoons maple syrup

60g ground almonds

2 teaspoons baking powder

1 teaspoon ground cinnamon

FOR THE FROSTING

150g 0% fat natural Greek yogurt

1 tablespoon maple syrup

15g pecan halves, toasted and roughly chopped

Cook's tip
Change the flavour by substituting ground hazelnuts for the ground almonds, and mixed spice instead of cinnamon.

6 **6** **5**

1 Preheat the oven to 180°C, fan 160°C, gas mark 4. Line 8 holes of a 12-hole muffin tin with paper cases.

2 Put the sweet potatoes in a microwave-safe bowl with 3 tablespoons water. Cover with clingfilm, pierce several holes in it and cook for 10-12 minutes on High until tender. Drain the cooked sweet potato, transfer to a mini food processor and blitz until smooth, or put in a bowl and mash using a potato masher.

3 In a mixing bowl, beat together the eggs, vegetable oil and maple syrup using a hand-held electric whisk until light and frothy. Fold in the almonds, baking powder, cinnamon and the cooled sweet potato until you have a smooth batter. Spoon the mixture into the paper cases.

4 Bake for 15-20 minutes or until firm to the touch. Remove from the oven, transfer to a wire rack and set aside to cool completely.

5 To make the frosting, fold the yogurt and the maple syrup together in a small bowl. Spoon on top of the cooled muffins, scatter over the chopped pecans, then serve.

Chocolate muffins

makes 6   prep time 5 minutes + cooling   cook time 20 minutes

3 1 1   122 kcal
per muffin

These no-fuss, four-ingredient muffins use bananas instead of added sugar and cocoa instead of flour. They're an excellent go-to when nothing but chocolate will do.

3 large very ripe bananas (about 450g peeled weight)

4 eggs, lightly beaten

4 tablespoons cocoa powder

20g dark chocolate (dairy free), to decorate

1 Preheat the oven to 180°C, fan 160°C, gas mark 4. Line 6 holes of a muffin tin with paper cases.

2 Put the bananas, eggs and cocoa powder in a food processor or blender and blitz until completely smooth. Divide the mixture between the paper cases and bake for 15-20 minutes or until a skewer inserted in the centre of a muffin comes out clean.

3 Transfer to a wire rack to cool completely. Put the chocolate in a microwave-safe bowl and microwave on High for 30 seconds or until melted. Drizzle the melted chocolate over the muffins, then allow to set before serving.

Cook's tip
Any time you have over-ripe bananas in the fruit bowl, simply pop them in the freezer, still in their skins. On defrosting, the flesh mashes very easily and is perfect for baking. This recipe is also easily scaled up – simply double the ingredients to make a full dozen.

Ricotta cheese scones

makes 12   **prep time 20 minutes**   **cook time 12 minutes**

4 **4** **4**   141 kcal per scone

Up your afternoon tea game with these cheesy savoury scones, which are seasoned with mustard powder, chives and black pepper.

320g self-raising flour, plus 10g for dusting

½ teaspoon baking powder

120g ricotta

40g vegetarian Italian-style hard cheese, finely grated

2 eggs

1 teaspoon ground black pepper

2 teaspoons mustard powder

1 tablespoon chopped fresh chives

Pinch of salt

150ml skimmed milk

1   Preheat the oven to 220°C, fan 200°C, gas mark 7. Line a baking sheet with baking paper.

2   Put the flour and baking powder in a large mixing bowl. In a separate bowl, beat together the ricotta, half the grated hard cheese, 1 egg, the pepper, mustard powder, chives and a pinch of salt. Add this mixture to the dry ingredients and mix well with just enough of the milk to form a soft dough.

3   Dust a work surface with the extra flour, turn out the dough and knead for 3 minutes. Roll out the dough to a thickness of 3cm, then stamp out 12 rounds with a 6cm pastry cutter – you will need to reroll the trimmings.

4   Beat the remaining egg in a small bowl. Put the scones on the prepared baking sheet, leaving room for them to expand, and brush the tops with the beaten egg. Sprinkle over the remaining grated hard cheese and bake for 10-12 minutes or until risen and golden.

Cook's tip

If you don't have mustard powder, you can substitute 1½ tablespoons of smooth mustard from a jar instead. The SmartPoints will stay the same.

Vegan choc chip cupcakes

makes 12   prep time 10 minutes   cook time 20 minutes

5 **5** **5**   130 kcal per cupcake

Both vegan and gluten-free, these are best served fresh out the oven, when the chunks of chocolate are still warm and melted.

Calorie controlled cooking spray

250ml unsweetened vanilla almond milk, at room temperature

1 tablespoon white wine vinegar

240g gluten-free self-raising flour

2 teaspoons baking powder

½ teaspoon salt

½ teaspoon bicarbonate of soda

60g light brown soft sugar

15g coconut oil, melted and cooled

1 teaspoon vanilla extract

60g vegan chocolate, chopped into very small pieces

1   Preheat the oven to 180°C, fan 160°C, gas mark 4. Mist a 12-hole cupcake or muffin tin with cooking spray.

2   Put the almond milk into a jug, add the vinegar and stir to combine. Set aside for 5 minutes while you prepare the other ingredients.

3   In a large bowl, sift together the flour, baking powder, salt and bicarbonate of soda, then stir in the sugar. Make a well in the centre of the mixture and add the almond milk mixture, coconut oil and vanilla. Stir until well combined. Reserve 20g of the chocolate to scatter over the tops before baking, then fold the rest into the batter.

4   Spoon the batter into the prepared muffin tin and scatter over the reserved chocolate. Bake for 20 minutes, until a skewer inserted into the centre of the cupcake comes out clean (it may have melted chocolate on it, but make sure it doesn't have raw batter clinging to it).

5   Serve warm, or cool on a wire rack before eating.

●   The cupcakes keep in an airtight container for up to 2 days but are best on the day of baking. If storing, warm them a little in the microwave before eating.

Cook's tip

Adding vinegar to the milk makes it curdle slightly; this acidity helps to activate the raising agents in the batter.

Apple & maple syrup cupcakes

makes 12 **prep time 20 minutes + cooling** **cook time 1 hour 20 minutes**

6 **6** **6**   187 kcal
per cupcake

The flavours of apple and maple syrup are a match made in heaven for these individual cakes topped with a cream cheese frosting.

2 apples, peeled, cored and finely chopped

125g low-fat spread

130g maple syrup

1 teaspoon vanilla extract

2 eggs

200g plain flour

1 teaspoon baking powder

1 teaspoon mixed spice

FOR THE FROSTING

100g low-fat soft cheese

30g low-fat spread

1½ tablespoons maple syrup

Pinch of mixed spice

FOR THE APPLE DECORATION

2 red apples, very thinly sliced, pips removed

Pinch of ground cinnamon, for dusting

Cook's tip

If you want to make the apple crisps ahead of time, they keep in an airtight container for up to 5 days.

1 Put the chopped apples in a pan with a splash of cold water. Cover and simmer over a moderate heat for 8-10 minutes until soft. Remove from the heat and roughly mash with the back of a fork. Leave to cool.

2 Preheat the oven to 190°C, fan 170°C, gas mark 5. Line a 12-hole muffin tin with paper cases. Put the spread, maple syrup and vanilla in a freestanding mixer and beat well until combined. Add the eggs, one at a time, and beat well between each addition.

3 Fold in the flour, baking powder and mixed spice until you have a smooth batter, then fold through the mashed apple.

4 Divide the mixture between the paper cases and bake for 20 minutes, or until risen and golden. Leave to cool completely.

5 Reduce the oven temperature to 120°C, fan 100°C, gas mark ½. For the decoration, line a baking tray with greaseproof paper, then lay the apple slices in a single layer. Dust with the cinnamon, then bake for 45 minutes to 1 hour until crisp. Set aside to cool and crisp up further.

6 Make the frosting. Whisk all the ingredients together in a bowl until well combined, then chill for 1 hour in the fridge to firm up. Spread over the cupcakes and top with a dried apple slice.

Banana & date biscotti

makes 18   **prep time 15 minutes + cooling**   **cook time 1 hour**

3 **3** **3**   89 kcal
per biscotti

Made for dunking in a hot drink, these double-baked Italian biscuits get their sweetness from fresh banana and dried dates.

180g wholemeal self-raising flour, plus 10g for dusting

2 tablespoons light brown soft sugar

60ml sunflower oil

1 egg, lightly beaten

1 large ripe banana, mashed (about 150g peeled weight)

40g dried dates, finely chopped

Cook's tip
Try adding 1 teaspoon mixed spice or ground ginger to give these a different flavour for the same SmartPoints.

1   Preheat the oven to 180°C, fan 160°C, gas mark 4, and line a large baking tray with baking paper.

2   Combine the flour and brown sugar in a mixing bowl. In a jug, combine the oil, egg and mashed banana. Pour the egg mixture into the flour mixture and mix to combine. Stir in the dates.

3   Dust your work surface with the extra flour and shape the dough into a 22cm-long log. Put onto the prepared tray and flatten slightly to a thickness of about 2cm. Bake for 30 minutes, or until firm. Let it cool on the tray.

4   Reduce the oven to 140°C, fan 120°C, gas mark 1. Using a sharp serrated knife, cut the log into 18 slices, about 1cm thick. Spread out, cut-side down, on the baking tray, then bake for 30 minutes or until crisp, turning halfway. Remove from the oven and cool on the tray.

●   The biscotti will keep in an airtight container for up to 2 weeks.

Chocolate oaty digestives

makes 12   **prep time 15 minutes + cooling**   **cook time 15 minutes**

(4) (3) (3)   87 kcal
per digestive

A great snack with a crisp crunch, these oat-packed biscuits can be coated with white, dark or milk chocolate – whichever you prefer.

40g low-fat spread

40g caster sugar

1 egg

½ teaspoon ground ginger

50g wholemeal plain flour

65g porridge oats

1 teaspoon baking powder

50g dark chocolate, chopped

1 Preheat the oven to 180°C, fan 160°C, gas mark 4. Line a baking sheet with baking paper.

2 In a large mixing bowl, cream together the spread and sugar using a hand-held electric whisk or wooden spoon. Beat in the egg, a little at a time, until combined.

3 In a separate bowl, combine the ginger, flour, oats and baking powder. Make a well in the centre and add the spread and egg mixture, then gently stir together – taking care not to overmix.

4 Spoon 12 walnut-size balls of the mixture onto the prepared baking sheet, leaving space between them to spread out, then flatten slightly with the back of the spoon. Bake for 12-15 minutes until golden brown. Allow to cool slightly, then transfer to a wire rack to cool completely.

Cook's tip

For a slightly chewier cookie-like result, switch to demerara or light brown soft sugar instead of caster, for the same SmartPoints.

5 When the biscuits have cooled, melt the chocolate in a heatproof bowl set over a pan of boiling water, or in the microwave. Dip one half of each biscuit in the melted chocolate, then return to the wire rack to set.

● The biscuits will keep in an airtight container for up to 4 days.

Chewy coconut cookies

makes 32 **prep time 20 minutes + cooling** **cook time 15 minutes**

3 **3** **3** 79 kcal
per cookie

These iconic Australian treats – also known as Anzac biscuits – are easy to make, keep well and call on ingredients you're likely to have in your storecupboard.

150g whole rolled oats

160g wholemeal plain flour

80g desiccated coconut

100g light brown soft sugar

125g low-fat spread

2 tablespoons golden syrup

1 teaspoon bicarbonate of soda

Cook's tip
Using wholemeal flour and whole rolled oats boosts the fibre content of these biscuits.

1 Preheat the oven to 180°C, fan 160°C, gas mark 4. Line 2 large baking trays with baking paper.

2 In a large bowl, combine the oats, flour, coconut and brown sugar. Put the spread and golden syrup in a small pan with 60ml water and heat over a medium-low heat. Cook, stirring, for 2-3 minutes or until melted and combined. Remove from the heat and stir in the bicarbonate of soda, which will make the mixture foam up. Pour into the flour mixture and stir to combine.

3 Using wet hands, roll tablespoonfuls of the mixture into balls and place on the prepared trays, spaced apart. Flatten the balls to about 5mm thickness and bake for 15 minutes or until crisp and golden. Set the biscuits aside on the trays for 5 minutes before transferring to a wire rack to cool.

Shortbread biscuits

makes 32   prep time 20 minutes + chilling   cook time 15 minutes

2 **2** **2** 65 kcal
per biscuit

There's nothing quite like homemade shortbread. These 'petticoat tails' are an attractive variation on the classic teatime favourite and make a great gift.

175g low-fat spread

75g caster sugar

1 egg

300g plain flour, plus 10g for dusting

1 teaspoon baking powder

Cook's tip
To make shortbread fingers, press the dough into a 20cm x 30cm baking tin, lined with baking paper. Mark into fingers with a knife before baking; cool in the tin then re-cut into fingers along the markings.

1 In a large mixing bowl, cream together the spread and sugar using a hand-held electric whisk or wooden spoon, then beat in the egg. Sift in the flour and the baking powder and combine until you have a stiff dough. Using your hands, press together into a ball, then wrap in clingfilm and chill in the freezer for 30 minutes to firm up.

2 Preheat the oven to 190°C, fan 170°C, gas mark 5.

3 Cut the dough in half. Put a piece of baking paper onto your work surface and dust with a little flour, then roll out one portion of the dough into a 22cm round on the baking paper. Using a fork, pierce the dough to mark out 16 equal segments – it helps if you mark it out in quarters first, then mark out each quarter into 4 more segments. Crimp the edge of the pastry round with your fingers, then lift the baking paper and dough onto a baking sheet.

4 Repeat with the remaining dough and place on a second baking sheet, then bake both rounds for 15 minutes, or until golden brown. Remove from the oven and transfer to a wire rack to cool. Cut into segments to serve.

Large cakes & traybakes

Forest fruit layer cake

serves 12   prep time 20 minutes + cooling   cook time 35 minutes

8 6 6   225 kcal
per serving

A gorgeous cake for a celebration with light sponges layered with a marbled berry-yogurt filling, crowned with a fruity compote.

Calorie controlled
cooking spray

150g low-fat spread

125g caster sugar

150g self-raising flour

1 teaspoon baking powder

4 large eggs

1 teaspoon vanilla extract

FOR THE COMPOTE

300g frozen mixed forest fruits

½ tablespoon vanilla extract

½ tablespoon clear honey

FOR THE FILLING/TOPPING

900g Skyr fat-free
natural yogurt

20g icing sugar, sifted

½ tablespoon vanilla extract

Cook's tip
Make sure that the sponges are fully cooled before you try to slice them; if they're still warm they will be fragile and likely to break. Store any leftovers in the fridge for up to 2 days.

1 Preheat the oven to 180°C, fan 160°C, gas mark 4. Mist 2 x 18cm-round cake tins with cooking spray and line with baking paper. Using an electric mixer, beat together the low-fat spread and caster sugar until pale and smooth.

2 Sift in the flour and baking powder, then add the eggs and 1 teaspoon vanilla and beat until just combined. Pour the mixture into the prepared tins, levelling the tops with the back of a spoon. Bake for 20-25 minutes, until a skewer inserted into the centre of the cake comes out clean. Set aside to cool slightly in the tins, then turn out onto a wire rack to cool completely.

3 Make the compote: put the compote ingredients in a pan with 1 teaspoon water and simmer over a low heat for 5 minutes until warm. Tip the mixture into a sieve set over a bowl to strain. Set aside the fruit. Return the juices to the pan and boil for 3-4 minutes, or until reduced slightly. Set aside to cool.

4 To make the filling/topping, whisk together the Skyr yogurt, icing sugar and vanilla in a bowl. Using a spoon, swirl the syrupy berry juices through the mixture.

5 Slice each cake in half horizontally to create four layers, then place one on a plate and spread over a quarter of the filling mixture. Repeat with the remaining cakes and filling, finishing with a layer of filling/topping. Spoon over the forest fruits and any remaining juice just before serving.

Cinnamon & pear cake

serves 8   prep time 20 minutes + cooling   cook time 40 minutes

(6) (6) (6)   157 kcal
per serving

Sweetly fragrant, this is the kind of cake that can be served still warm for pudding, or completely cooled with a hot cuppa for afternoon tea.

Calorie controlled cooking spray

75g low-fat spread

80g caster sugar

1 egg

2 teaspoons vanilla extract

½ teaspoon ground cinnamon

140g self-raising flour, sifted

½ teaspoon baking powder

80ml skimmed milk

1 medium pear, sliced into thin wedges

1   Preheat the oven to 180°C, fan 160°C, gas mark 4. Mist a 20cm springform tin with cooking spray and line the base with baking paper. Reserve 2 teaspoons spread and 2 teaspoons sugar for the topping.

2   Using a hand-held electric whisk, beat the remaining spread and sugar with the egg, vanilla extract and half of the cinnamon in a bowl, until combined. Stir in half of the flour, the baking powder, then all of the milk. Stir in the remaining flour until combined. Spoon the mixture into the prepared tin and use a spatula to level the surface. Arrange the pear slices on top in a circular pattern.

3   Bake for 30-40 minutes or until a skewer inserted into the centre of the cake comes out clean. Cool the cake in the tin for 5 minutes, then release from the tin and transfer to a wire rack.

4   Melt the reserved spread in the microwave and brush all over the hot cake. Combine the remaining cinnamon and reserved sugar in a small bowl, then sprinkle this over the cake before slicing and serving.

Cook's tip
Use a slightly under-ripe pear so that it slices neatly for the decorative top.

Coffee meringue cake

serves 12   prep time 15 minutes + cooling   cook time 35 minutes

8 **8** **8**   167 kcal per serving

A coffee enthusiast's dream: this cake has a sublime combination of coffee sponge, chocolate mascarpone filling and crisp-yet-soft meringue.

Calorie controlled cooking spray

100g low-fat spread

80g caster sugar

2 eggs, beaten

100g self-raising flour

½ teaspoon baking powder

1 teaspoon instant coffee, dissolved in 1 tablespoon boiling water, cooled

FOR THE MERINGUE

2 egg whites

100g caster sugar

1 teaspoon instant coffee, dissolved in 1 tablespoon boiling water, cooled

FOR THE FILLING

4 teaspoons cocoa powder

80g low-fat mascarpone

50g icing sugar

Cook's tip

Make sure that both the sponge and meringue are completely cool before assembling, or the filling will melt.

1   Preheat the oven to 180°C, fan 160°C, gas mark 4. Mist a 20cm round cake tin with cooking spray and line with baking paper. Draw an 18cm circle on a separate sheet of baking paper, then place it on a baking sheet.

2   Make the meringue. In a large bowl, whisk the egg whites, using a hand-held electric whisk, to soft peak stage. Add the caster sugar, a spoonful at a time; continue whisking until stiff peaks form. Gently fold in the cooled coffee. Spoon the meringue onto the baking paper sheet. Spread out to fill the 18cm circle with a spatula, creating some swirls and peaks. Set aside while you make the cake.

3   To make the cake, beat the spread and sugar in a bowl until creamy. Gradually beat in the eggs until well combined. Gently fold in the flour, baking powder and coffee, then pour the batter into the prepared tin.

4   Bake the cake and meringue for 20 minutes. Insert a skewer into the centre of the cake – if it comes out clean, the cake is cooked. Remove from the oven and set aside to cool in the tin for 10 minutes, then turn out onto a wire rack to cool completely. Continue to cook the meringue for a further 10-15 minutes until crisp. Remove from the oven and set aside to cool; it will spread out slightly so that it is the same size as the top of the cake.

5   Make the filling. Set aside ¼ teaspoon cocoa, then add the rest to a bowl with the mascarpone and icing sugar. Beat until smooth. Spread over the cooled sponge and top with the coffee meringue. Dust with the reserved cocoa.

Strawberry Bakewell cake

serves 10   prep time 15 minutes + cooling   cook time 50 minutes

(6) (5) (5)   192 kcal per serving   (icon)

Just the thing for warm-weather picnics, this easy-to-transport almond-flavoured sponge is baked with a fragrant strawberry and crunchy flaked almond topping.

Calorie controlled cooking spray

2 x 400g tins cannellini beans, drained and rinsed

125ml agave syrup

100g low-fat spread

2 large eggs, plus 2 large egg whites

100g plain flour

2 teaspoons baking powder

1 teaspoon vanilla extract

1 teaspoon almond extract

175g fresh strawberries, hulled and halved

5g flaked almonds

1 teaspoon icing sugar, to decorate

Cook's tip

For a more traditional Bakewell, try the same quantity of fresh pitted cherries instead of strawberries, when in season.

1   Preheat the oven to 180°C, fan 160°C, gas mark 4. Mist a 20cm springform or loose-bottomed cake tin with cooking spray and line the base and sides with baking paper.

2   Put the cannellini beans, agave syrup and low-fat spread in a food processor and blitz until smooth. Transfer to a large mixing bowl, whisk in the whole eggs, one at a time, then whisk in the egg whites.

3   Fold in the flour, baking powder and vanilla and almond extracts, then pour the mixture into the prepared tin. Arrange the strawberries, cut-side up, on top and scatter over the flaked almonds.

4   Bake for 45-50 minutes or until a skewer inserted into the centre of the cake comes out clean. Leave to cool in the tin for 10 minutes, then carefully remove from the tin and transfer to a wire rack to cool completely. Dust with the icing sugar, then cut into slices and serve.

Citrus upside-down cake

serves 12   prep time 20 minutes + cooling   cook time 50 minutes

7 **6** **6**   181 kcal
per serving

Glossy slices of caramelised orange are baked into this topsy-turvy bake, which is then glazed with the sticky syrup to serve.

Calorie controlled cooking spray

2 oranges

160g caster sugar

1 blood orange, very thinly sliced (or another regular orange)

160g low-fat spread

3 eggs

1 teaspoon vanilla extract

160g self-raising flour

Cook's tip

For a speedier cake without the sliced orange topping and syrup, spread 100g low-calorie marmalade in the base of the lined tin before adding the cake mixture; this will give a sticky glaze to the cake when turned out.

6 **5** **5**

1   Preheat the oven to 180°C, fan 160°C, gas mark 4. Mist a 20cm square cake tin with cooking spray and line with baking paper.

2   Grate the zest from the 2 oranges, then thinly slice one and squeeze the juice from the other (you'll need 60ml juice). Put 100g of the sugar in a large frying pan with 50ml water. Heat over a gentle heat, stirring, until the sugar has dissolved. Turn up the heat and add the sliced orange and the blood orange. Simmer for 10-15 minutes, or until the orange slices are soft and the liquid is syrupy. Using a slotted spoon, remove the fruit from the pan; set aside to cool. Stir the orange juice into the liquid in the pan, then set aside.

3   In a large mixing bowl, cream together the remaining 60g sugar and the spread using a hand-held electric whisk. Add the eggs, one at a time, beating between each addition. Add the orange zest and vanilla and stir well to incorporate. Gently fold in the flour until you have a smooth batter.

4   Arrange the orange slices over the base of the prepared tin, then pour over the cake mixture. Bake for 30-35 minutes, or until golden and a skewer inserted into the centre of the cake comes out clean. Remove from the oven and set aside to cool in the tin.

5   Turn the cake out onto a serving plate and remove the baking paper. Brush the orange syrup over the top of the cake, then slice and serve.

Chocolate courgette brownies

makes 20   prep time 30 minutes + cooling   cook time 1 hour 25 minutes

6 6 6   142 kcal
per brownie

Friends and family will never guess that grated courgette is the secret ingredient that gives these decadent, chocolatey treats a lovely moist texture.

Calorie controlled cooking spray

150g dark chocolate, roughly chopped

175g low-fat spread, cut into cubes

3 eggs

175g caster sugar

150g wholemeal self-raising flour

275g grated courgette (about 1 large courgette)

1 teaspoon cocoa powder, to decorate

Cook's tip

For an intense chocolate hit, look for a dark chocolate that contains at least 70% cocoa solids.

1 Preheat the oven to 180°C, fan 160°C, gas mark 4. Mist a 20cm square tin with cooking spray and line with baking paper, leaving some paper hanging over the edge of the tin to make it easy to lift out.

2 Put the chocolate and the spread in a heatproof bowl set over a pan of gently boiling water, making sure the water isn't high enough to touch the bowl. Stir occasionally until the chocolate and spread have melted, then remove from the heat and set aside.

3 In a separate bowl, whisk the eggs and sugar together using a hand-held electric whisk for a few minutes until thick. Pour in the melted chocolate and spread, then fold together until combined. Gently fold in the flour, followed by the grated courgette.

4 Pour the mixture into the prepared tin and smooth the top with a spatula. Bake for 1 hour 15 minutes, until only a few crumbs remain when you insert a skewer into the centre of the brownie.

5 Remove from the oven and put the tin on a wire rack. Leave until completely cool, then use the baking paper to lift the brownie out of the tin. Remove the baking paper, dust the top with the cocoa powder and cut into 20 individual brownies.

Raspberry & coconut slice

serves 16   prep time 15 minutes + cooling   cook time 30 minutes

4 **4** **4**   119 kcal
per serving

A made-in-minutes oats and coconut mixture doubles up as both a crunchy base and a crumble topping for these fruity berry squares.

Calorie controlled cooking spray

200g plain flour

60g caster sugar

50g porridge oats

40g desiccated coconut

Pinch of salt

130g low-fat spread

250g raspberries

1 Preheat the oven to 190°C, fan 170°C, gas mark 5. Mist a 22cm square cake tin with cooking spray and line with baking paper.

2 In a large mixing bowl, combine the flour, sugar, oats and coconut with a pinch of salt. Add the spread and rub it into the dry ingredients with your fingertips until combined and the mixture resembles coarse crumbs.

3 Press half the mixture into the prepared tin. Top with the raspberries, pressing down gently with a spatula to release some of the juice. Scatter over the remaining oat mixture and smooth with a spatula – it doesn't matter if some of the raspberries are peeking through.

4 Bake for 30 minutes or until golden brown. Remove from the oven and set aside to cool in the tin for 1 hour, then turn out onto a chopping board and remove the baking paper. Cut into squares to serve.

Cook's tip

Switch the raspberries for blueberries and add the zest of 1 lime for a different flavour, with the same SmartPoints. You can easily make this recipe gluten-free; simply use gluten-free plain flour and oats instead of regular.

Marshmallow squares

makes 16   **prep time 10 minutes + chilling**   **cook time 10 minutes**

3 **3** **3**   61 kcal
per square

A retro-style favourite, this no-bake sweet and sticky treat is made with just three ingredients and one pan.

50g low-fat spread
165g mini marshmallows
65g puffed rice

1   Line a 20cm square cake tin with baking paper, leaving some paper hanging over the edge of the tin to make it easy to lift out.

2   In a large pan, melt the spread over a low heat. Add 150g of the marshmallows and cook for about 10 minutes, stirring often, until the marshmallows have melted and the mixture is smooth and combined.

3   Remove from the heat and stir in the puffed rice, mixing well so it is completely coated in the sticky marshmallow mixture.

Cook's tip
Make sure to keep stirring the marshmallows as they melt, so that they don't catch and burn on the bottom of the pan. Low and slow is the key; don't try to rush the process.

4   While the mixture is still warm, spoon it into the prepared tin and press lightly with a spatula to smooth the top. Scatter over the remaining marshmallows, then chill for at least 30 minutes to set. Lift out of the tin onto a chopping board and remove the baking paper, then cut into 16 squares and serve.

Chocolate cake with sweet potato frosting

serves 18   **prep time 30 minutes + soaking and cooling**   **cook time 45 minutes**

7 **7** **6**   170 kcal per serving

Mashed sweet potato forms the basis of a fabulously fudgy chocolate-orange icing for this clever bake, while date purée adds natural sweetness to the sponge.

Calorie controlled cooking spray

200g pitted Medjool dates, halved

50g cocoa powder

100g low-fat spread

3 eggs

200g self-raising flour

1½ teaspoons baking powder

100ml semi-skimmed milk

2 teaspoons vanilla extract

FOR THE SWEET POTATO FROSTING

300g cooked sweet potato

100g dark chocolate, roughly chopped

50g milk chocolate, roughly chopped

Zest of ½ orange, plus 1 tablespoon of juice

Cook's tip
You can bake the sweet potato ahead of time, or simply peel, chop and microwave in a covered bowl until tender. Drain, cool and mash to a purée.

1 Preheat the oven to 180°C, fan 160°C, gas mark 4. Mist a 28cm x 18cm cake tin with cooking spray and line with baking paper.

2 Put the dates in a heatproof bowl, cover with hot water and set aside to soak for 30 minutes until softened. Drain then blitz in a food processor until smooth.

3 In a small bowl, blend the cocoa powder to a paste with 6 tablespoons boiling water. Transfer to a large mixing bowl, add the spread and beat until smooth. Add the date purée and beat to combine, then add the eggs, one at a time, beating well after each addition. Sift the flour and baking powder into the bowl; fold until just combined. Finally, fold in the milk and vanilla extract.

4 Spoon the mixture into the prepared tin, level the top and bake for 40-45 minutes, or until risen and firm to the touch. Cool in the tin for 10 minutes, then turn out onto a cooling rack to cool completely.

5 To make the frosting, heat the sweet potato and both types of chocolate in a pan over a low heat, stirring until the chocolate has melted and the mixture is smooth and combined. Put in a food processor, add the orange zest and juice and blitz until smooth. Spoon into a bowl and let cool to room temperature. Spread over the cake, then serve.

● The cake will keep in an airtight container for up to 2 days.

Lamington traybake

serves 20   prep time 40 minutes + cooling and chilling   cook time 20 minutes

(6) (6) (6)   139 kcal per serving   (icons)

An Australian classic in traybake form, this sponge cake is layered with a sweetened ricotta and chia seed 'jam' then spread with chocolate icing and topped with coconut.

Calorie controlled cooking spray

6 eggs

100g caster sugar

½ teaspoon vanilla extract

75g self-raising flour

50g cornflour

50g plain flour

FOR THE 'JAM'

220g frozen raspberries, thawed

1 tablespoon chia seeds

10g icing sugar

FOR THE FILLING

200g ricotta

½ teaspoon vanilla extract

10g icing sugar

FOR THE TOPPING

150g icing sugar

20g cocoa powder

2 tablespoons skimmed milk

40g desiccated coconut

Cook's tip
If you only have one tin, make and bake the sponge mixture in two batches.

1 Preheat the oven to 180°C, fan 160°C, gas mark 4. Lightly mist 2 x 20cm x 30cm baking tins with cooking spray and line with baking paper, allowing some overhang.

2 To make the 'jam', press the raspberries and any juices through a sieve set over a small pan. Discard the seeds. Stir in the chia and icing sugar. Cook over a medium heat for 3 minutes. Remove from the heat to cool and thicken.

3 For the cake, beat the eggs, sugar and vanilla together in a bowl, until the mixture is pale and doubled in size. Sift in the flours and fold to combine. Divide between the tins. Bake for 15 minutes, until springy. Cool in the tins for 5 minutes, then turn out onto a rack to cool completely.

4 Meanwhile, for the filling, whisk the ricotta, vanilla and icing sugar in a bowl until smooth. Cover and chill until needed.

5 To assemble, mist and line one of the cake tins as before. Place one sponge in the tin and spread with the ricotta mixture, followed by the 'jam'. Invert the second sponge on top, cover with baking paper and place another tin on top, weighing it down with 2 full tin cans. Chill for 1 hour.

6 For the topping, sift the icing sugar and cocoa into a heatproof bowl set over a pan of simmering water, then mix in the milk. Stir for 2-3 minutes until warm. Spread over the sponge and scatter on the coconut. Allow to set.

7 To serve, use the overhanging baking paper to carefully lift the slice out of the tin, then cut into squares.

Pear & cranberry streusel bars

makes 12   prep time 10 minutes + cooling   cook time 20 minutes

(5) (5) (4)   165 kcal
per bar

Streusel is the German term for a crumble topping – often with nuts added for extra crunch – that's sprinkled on top of muffins and cakes before baking.

Calorie controlled cooking spray

50g low-fat spread

75g clear honey

200g porridge oats

50g ground almonds

½ teaspoon almond extract

2 medium pears, peeled, cored and chopped

100g fresh or frozen cranberries

FOR THE STREUSEL TOPPING

25g low-fat spread

25g plain flour

15g flaked almonds

1 tablespoon demerara sugar

1 Preheat the oven to 220°C, fan 200°C, gas mark 7. Mist a 15cm x 23cm baking tin with cooking spray, and line with baking paper.

2 Put the spread and honey in a large pan over a low heat. Gently heat until the spread has melted. Remove from the heat and stir in the oats, ground almonds and almond extract until combined, then gently stir in the pears and cranberries. Spoon into the prepared tin and press down firmly with the back of a spoon.

3 To make the streusel topping, use your fingers to rub the spread and flour together in a bowl. Stir in the flaked almonds and sugar. Scatter over the fruity oat mixture in the tin and press on lightly. Bake for 10-15 minutes or until firm and golden brown. Leave to cool completely in the tin then cut into 12 bars.

● The bars will keep in an airtight container for up to 3 days.

Cook's tip
These transport really well. Wrap a bar and pop it in your bag for a delicious breakfast or snack on the go.

Tottenham cake

serves 16   prep time 25 minutes + cooling   cook time 20 minutes

8 8 8   181 kcal per serving

A traditional favourite, this used to be sold to children for a penny a slice in the 1800s. The vivid pink icing is naturally coloured using raspberry juice.

Calorie controlled cooking spray

170g low-fat spread

170g caster sugar

3 eggs, lightly beaten

1 teaspoon vanilla extract

1 teaspoon lemon zest

225g plain flour

2 teaspoons baking powder

FOR THE ICING

70g raspberries

150g icing sugar

Cook's tip

Try using blueberries instead of raspberries to get a slightly deeper pink icing for the same SmartPoints.

1 Preheat the oven to 180°C, fan 160°C, gas mark 4. Mist a 32cm x 22cm traybake tin with cooking spray and line with baking paper. Cream the spread and sugar together in a large mixing bowl. Gradually beat in the eggs, then add the vanilla extract and lemon zest.

2 Sift in the flour and baking powder, then fold in gently. Pour into the prepared tin. Bake for 15-18 minutes, until golden brown and springy to the touch. Leave in the tin until completely cool, then transfer to a wire rack.

3 To make the icing, put the raspberries and 2 tablespoons water in a small pan over a low-medium heat and cook for 5 minutes until they start to break down. Remove from the heat. Using the back of a spoon, press through a sieve into a small bowl, gently squeezing out all the juice. Put 130g of the icing sugar in a bowl. Gradually mix in the raspberry juice until you have a thick, spreadable icing. In a separate bowl, combine the remaining icing sugar with 1 teaspoon water to make a slightly thinner white icing.

4 Spoon the pink icing over the cake and smooth out with a palette knife. Pour the white icing into a small piping bag; snip off the end to give a small opening and pipe the icing in parallel lines across the cake, about 3cm apart. Drag a cocktail stick or skewer in the opposite direction, to create a feathered look. Leave to set completely at room temperature before slicing and serving.

Rocky road bites

makes 20　　**prep time 10 minutes + cooling and chilling**　　**cook time 1 minute**

3　**3**　**3**　71 kcal
per bite

When you want just a little sweet treat that will appeal to all the family, these easy no-bake bites are sure to hit the spot.

50g low-fat spread

150g dark chocolate, broken into pieces

50g mini marshmallows

70g reduced-fat rich tea biscuits, crushed into small pieces

1　Line an 18cm square cake tin (or baking dish) with baking paper, leaving some paper hanging over the edge of the tin to make it easy to lift out. Put the spread and chocolate in a large microwave-safe bowl and heat in the microwave for 1 minute, or until melted. Set aside for 5 minutes to cool slightly.

2　Reserve a few of the marshmallows for decoration, then add the rest to the chocolate mixture, along with the biscuits, and stir well to combine. Spoon the mixture into the prepared tin and smooth the top with a spatula. Scatter over the reserved marshmallows and chill for 1 hour or until set.

3　Lift the rocky road out of the tin, remove the baking paper and cut into 20 equal pieces.

Cook's tip
Change the flavours by replacing the dark chocolate with white, and use the same quantity of WW Malt Chocolate Balls instead of rich tea biscuits, for the same SmartPoints.

Mango, blueberry & lime traybake

serves 12   prep time 15 minutes + cooling   cook time 30 minutes

(6) (5) (4)   167 kcal per serving   (v) (gf)

Tropical flavours provide plenty of zing in this super-simple dairy-free bake, which is made using creamy nut butter and a tin of chickpeas.

Calorie controlled cooking spray

400g tin chickpeas, drained and rinsed

100g smooth cashew butter, or smooth almond butter

75g maple syrup

2 eggs

2 teaspoons vanilla extract

Zest of 1 lime, plus 1 teaspoon juice

75g porridge oats

25g desiccated coconut

1 teaspoon baking powder

100g blueberries

100g ripe mango, diced

TO DECORATE

50g icing sugar, sifted

Zest of 1 lime, plus 1 teaspoon juice

1 Preheat the oven to 180°C, fan 160°C, gas mark 4. Mist a 20cm square shallow baking tin with cooking spray and line with baking paper.

2 Blitz the chickpeas in a food processor with the nut butter, maple syrup, eggs, vanilla extract, lime zest and juice, until combined. Spoon into a bowl, add the oats, coconut and baking powder and mix well. Fold through the blueberries and mango, then pour into the prepared tin and level the surface. Bake for 30 minutes, or until risen and golden.

3 Remove from the oven and cool in the tin for 10 minutes. Turn out onto a wire rack to cool completely.

4 Mix the icing sugar and lime juice with 2 teaspoons water until smooth and combined. Drizzle the icing over the traybake then scatter over the lime zest and cut into squares to serve.

Cook's tip
Use gluten-free oats for a gluten-free bake.

Apple & sultana cake

serves 12   prep time 15 minutes + cooling   cook time 35 minutes

(5) (4) (4)   136 kcal
per serving

If you love apple pie, you'll be a firm fan of this easy traybake that's sweetened with honey and flavoured with warming mixed spice.

Calorie controlled cooking spray

4 large eggs

4 tablespoons clear honey, plus 1 teaspoon for brushing

75g low-fat natural yogurt

200g self-raising flour

1 teaspoon mixed spice

50g sultanas

2 large red apples, cored and thinly sliced

1   Preheat the oven to 180°C, fan 160°C, gas mark 4. Mist a 20cm square tin with cooking spray and line with baking paper.

2   In a large bowl, whisk together the eggs, honey and yogurt. Gently fold in the flour and mixed spice until all of the ingredients are combined and you have a smooth batter. Stir in the sultanas and most of the apple slices, reserving about 15 slices for decoration.

3   Pour the mixture into the prepared tin and smooth the top with a spatula. Top with the reserved apple slices, then bake for 30-35 minutes, or until the top is golden brown and a skewer inserted into the centre of the cake comes out clean.

4   Remove from the oven and brush over the extra 1 teaspoon honey. Leave to cool for 10 minutes, then turn out onto a wire rack to cool completely. Remove the baking paper, then slice and serve.

Cook's tip
Shake up the flavours by swapping the apples for pears, and switching the mixed spice to ground ginger. The SmartPoints will remain the same.

Blueberry yogurt cake

serves 12 **prep time 20 minutes + cooling** **cook time 55 minutes**

(7) (6) (6) 176 kcal per serving

Pops of blueberry and tangy lemon zest combine beautifully in this simple loaf cake, which is finished with a juicy blueberry compote.

Calorie controlled cooking spray

125g low-fat spread

150g caster sugar

3 eggs

100g low-fat natural yogurt

Grated zest of 1 lemon

1 teaspoon vanilla extract

200g self-raising flour

250g blueberries

1 teaspoon icing sugar, to decorate

Cook's tip
You can use either fresh or frozen blueberries to make this loaf. There's no need to defrost them if you're using frozen; just add them to the batter straight from the pack. For a flavour twist, try with raspberries or mixed summer fruits instead.

1 Preheat the oven to 180°C, fan 160°C, gas mark 4. Mist a 900g loaf tin with cooking spray and line with baking paper or a paper loaf tin liner.

2 Put the spread, caster sugar, eggs, yogurt, lemon zest and vanilla extract in a bowl, and whisk until combined. Gently fold in the flour until you have a smooth batter, then add half the blueberries and stir to combine.

3 Pour the mixture into the prepared loaf tin and bake for 45-50 minutes, or until well risen and a skewer inserted into the centre of the cake comes out clean. Remove from the oven and leave to cool in the tin for 10 minutes, then turn out onto a wire rack and leave to cool completely.

4 Meanwhile, put the remaining blueberries in a pan and cover with a lid. Cook over a low heat for approximately 5 minutes, or until they are soft and have started to release their juice. Set aside to cool.

5 When the cake is completely cool, remove the paper liner and spoon the blueberry compote over the top. Dust with the icing sugar, then slice and serve.

Marbled chocolate & banana loaf

serves 12 **prep time 15 minutes + cooling** **cook time 1 hour**

6 **6** **6** 187 kcal per serving

A great way to use up any bananas that have gone past their best in the fruit bowl, a slice of this loaf cake goes down well with a cup of coffee.

Calorie controlled cooking spray

25g cocoa powder

450g ripe bananas (unpeeled weight), mashed

2 eggs, beaten

½ teaspoon vanilla extract

225g self-raising flour

110g low-fat spread

110g light brown soft sugar

1   Preheat the oven to 180°C, fan 160°C, gas mark 4. Mist a 900g loaf tin with cooking spray and line with baking paper or a paper loaf tin liner. Sift the cocoa into a heatproof bowl, add 4 tablespoons boiling water and stir to a smooth paste. Set aside to cool.

2   Mix the bananas, eggs and vanilla in a bowl. Sift the flour into a separate bowl and rub in the spread with your fingers. Stir the sugar into the flour mixture, then add the banana mixture and stir until well combined. Transfer a third of this to the bowl holding the cocoa mixture and stir until well combined.

3   Spoon random dollops of each mixture into the prepared tin until you've used all the mixture, then swirl with a knife for a marbled effect.

4   Bake for 50 minutes to 1 hour until risen and golden and a skewer inserted into the centre of the loaf comes out clean. Leave to cool in the tin for 10 minutes, then turn out onto a wire rack to cool before slicing and serving.

Cook's tip

Add a chocolate glaze: sift 15g cocoa powder and 15g icing sugar into a small bowl, then stir in 1½ tablespoons hot water from the kettle. Drizzle over the cooled loaf. The SmartPoints will stay the same.

Butternut squash cake

serves 12   prep time 20 minutes + cooling   cook time 2 hours

7 **7** **7**   191 kcal
per serving

Aromatic orange zest and fresh rosemary boost the flavour of this lovely loaf cake, which is finished with a drizzle of orange icing.

Calorie controlled
cooking spray

½ butternut squash, about
450g, seeds removed

1 sprig fresh rosemary, leaves
removed and finely chopped,
plus an extra sprig to decorate

125g low-fat spread

100g light brown soft sugar

3 large eggs

250g self-raising flour

Grated zest and juice
of 1 orange

50g icing sugar

Cook's tip

Save time and get ahead
by roasting the squash
when you already have the
oven on to cook a meal.
The roast squash purée
will keep in the fridge for
about three days.

1 Preheat the oven to 200°C, fan 180°C, gas mark 6. Mist a 900g loaf tin with cooking spray and line with baking paper or a paper loaf tin liner. Put the squash in a roasting tin and mist with cooking spray, then sprinkle over the chopped rosemary. Roast for 45 minutes, or until tender. Cool slightly, then scoop out 300g of the roasted flesh and purée with either a stick blender or potato masher.

2 In a large mixing bowl, beat together the spread and brown sugar using a hand-held electric whisk until light and fluffy. Beat in the eggs, one at a time, adding a spoonful of the flour with each egg. Gently fold the remaining flour, orange zest and butternut purée into the mixture.

3 Spoon the mixture into the prepared tin and bake for 1 hour 15 minutes, or until a skewer inserted into the centre of the cake comes out clean. Cover the cake with kitchen foil towards the end of cooking time if it is browning too much. Leave to cool in the tin for a few minutes, then turn out onto a wire rack to cool completely.

4 To decorate, mix the icing sugar with 2 teaspoons of the orange juice. Beat until smooth, adding a little more juice if needed. Drizzle over the top of the cake, decorate with the extra rosemary sprig, then slice and serve.

Bread, pastries & desserts

Herby focaccia

serves 16   prep time 20 minutes + proving and cooling   cook time 30 minutes

5 **5** **5**   151 kcal
                        per serving

This aromatic gluten-free version of the Italian-style bread uses xanthan gum (available in most supermarkets) to give the loaf its characteristic springy texture.

200ml semi-skimmed milk

2 eggs

4½ tablespoons olive oil

1 tablespoon clear honey

400g gluten-free white bread flour

7g sachet fast-action dried yeast

1½ teaspoons xanthan gum

2 teaspoons cider vinegar

¼ teaspoon bicarbonate of soda

3 sprigs fresh rosemary

3 sprigs fresh thyme, cut into smaller sprigs

1 tablespoon flaky or coarse sea salt

Cook's tip

Scatter the focaccia with a handful of halved cherry tomatoes before baking. The SmartPoints will remain the same.

1 Preheat the oven to 200°C, fan 180°C, gas mark 6. Gently heat the milk in a small pan over a low heat, until it's warm to the touch, but not hot. Put the eggs, 2 tablespoons of the oil and the honey into a bowl, and whisk in the warmed milk.

2 In a large mixing bowl, combine the flour, yeast and xanthan gum, and make a well in the centre. Pour the milk mixture into the well and stir everything together to form a sticky dough.

3 In a small jug, combine the vinegar with the bicarbonate of soda and immediately add it to the dough, mixing thoroughly. Grease a baking sheet with ½ tablespoon of the oil and, using wet fingers, stretch and smooth the dough onto the baking sheet right up into the corners. Brush a little of the remaining oil over a sheet of clingfilm, then use to cover the dough. Set aside in a warm place for 1½ hours, or until doubled in size.

4 Once risen, use your fingers or the end of a wooden spoon, dipped in gluten-free flour, to make random holes in the dough. Poke small sprigs of the herbs in each hole, drizzle the entire loaf with the remaining olive oil and sprinkle over the sea salt. Bake for 25-30 minutes or until golden and cooked through. Serve warm.

Cinnamon rolls

makes 15   prep time 15 minutes + cooling   cook time 25 minutes

6 **5** **5**   166 kcal
per roll

Just the thing for a celebratory breakfast or brunch; these will fill your home
with a wonderful fragrance as they bake.

**450g self-raising flour, plus
10g for dusting**

20g icing sugar

2 teaspoons baking powder

Pinch of salt

**360g 0% fat natural
Greek yogurt**

1 tablespoon vanilla extract

1 large egg

**Calorie controlled
cooking spray**

20g low-fat spread, melted

40g light brown soft sugar

1 tablespoon ground cinnamon

FOR THE GLAZE

60g icing sugar, sifted

40g 0% fat natural Greek yogurt

¼ teaspoon vanilla extract

Cook's tip
Make these Scandi-style
by adding ½ teaspoon
ground cardamom to the
dough, with the flour.

1   Preheat the oven to 180°C, fan 160°C, gas mark 4. In a
large bowl, mix together the flour, icing sugar and baking
powder with a pinch of salt, then set aside. In a medium
bowl, whisk together the yogurt, vanilla and egg until
combined. Add the yogurt mixture to the flour mixture;
stir well with a wooden spoon until just combined and
then knead the mixture in the bowl for 2 minutes.

2   Tip the dough onto a work surface and knead the mixture
for 2 minutes, until smooth, dusting with the extra flour
if needed. Transfer the dough to a large piece of baking
paper that's misted with cooking spray. Roll out the
dough to a rectangle about 38cm x 23cm.

3   Brush the dough all over with the melted spread.
Combine the brown sugar and cinnamon, then sprinkle
this all over the dough. Starting with a long edge, roll
up tightly to form a long roll. Cut the roll into 15 x 2.5cm
slices. Arrange in a medium rectangular baking dish
that's been misted with cooking spray, leaving a little
room between them to expand. Bake for 20-25 minutes,
until risen and lightly browned. Let them stand for
10 minutes in the dish, to cool slightly.

4   Meanwhile, make the glaze. Combine the icing sugar,
yogurt and vanilla, stirring until smooth. Drizzle the glaze
over the warm cinnamon rolls and serve.

Soda bread

serves 14   **prep time 10 minutes + cooling**   **cook time 30 minutes**

4 **4** **3**   129 kcal per serving

A super-quick and easy loaf, this uses bicarbonate of soda rather than yeast so it's a simple mix-and-bake recipe; no kneading or rising time required.

200g wholemeal self-raising flour, plus 10g for dusting

200g plain flour

½ teaspoon bicarbonate of soda

60g jumbo oats

1 teaspoon salt

1 tablespoon dark brown soft sugar

350ml buttermilk

Calorie controlled cooking spray

1 Preheat the oven to 220°C, fan 200°C, gas mark 7. Put a medium casserole dish with the lid on in the oven to heat while you prepare the dough.

2 Sift both flours and the bicarbonate of soda into a large mixing bowl and add in any bran that's left behind in the sieve. Mix in 50g of the oats, the salt and sugar, then stir through the buttermilk to form a sticky dough.

3 Turn out onto a lightly floured surface and form into a large round loaf. Dip the handle of a wooden spoon into some flour and use it to gently press a cross into the top of the loaf.

4 Remove the heated casserole dish from the oven and mist with cooking spray, then carefully transfer the dough to the casserole. Scatter over the remaining oats, then cover with the lid and bake for 25-30 minutes or until the loaf is risen and golden. Leave for 15 minutes in the casserole dish, then transfer to a wire rack to cool completely.

Cook's tip

Mix grated lemon zest and finely chopped fresh thyme or rosemary into low-fat spread to serve with the soda bread; make sure to allow extra SmartPoints for the low-fat spread.

Pizza loaf

serves 12   **prep time 45 minutes + proving and cooling**   **cook time 40 minutes**

(4) (4) (4)   137 kcal per serving

Do the twist with this savoury loaf, filled with olives, sun-dried tomatoes, aromatic basil and chunks of gooey mozzarella; lovely served with a ZeroPoint soup.

250g strong white bread flour, plus 10g for dusting

1 teaspoon salt

½ teaspoon caster sugar

3g fast-action dried yeast

1½ tablespoons olive oil, plus ½ teaspoon for greasing

50g pitted green olives, roughly chopped

70g sun-dried tomatoes in oil, drained and roughly chopped

Small handful fresh basil, roughly chopped

125g light mozzarella, torn into small chunks

1 egg, lightly beaten

Cook's tip
Instead of a twist, try making a 'Stromboli' loaf; simply transfer the filled and rolled dough to a lined baking tray and snip little holes along the top, so that the cheese can bubble out during cooking.

1   Sift the flour into a large mixing bowl and add the salt, sugar and yeast. Make a well in the centre, then pour in 120ml warm water and the oil, and mix to form a soft dough. Add a little extra warm water if the dough is too dry.

2   Turn the dough out onto a lightly floured work surface and knead for 7-10 minutes, or until it is smooth and elastic. Transfer to a lightly oiled bowl, cover with a tea towel and leave in a warm place for 1 hour or until doubled in size.

3   Meanwhile, combine the green olives with the sun-dried tomatoes, basil and some freshly ground black pepper.

4   Turn the dough out onto a lightly floured work surface. Knock out the air by kneading for a couple of minutes. Roll into a 36cm x 22cm rectangle. Spread over the tomato and olive mixture and dot with the mozzarella. Starting from the longest edge, roll the dough tightly into a sausage shape. Cut in half lengthways, but leave 3cm uncut at one end so the two halves are attached. Twist the two halves together like a rope, letting the filling show. Pinch the ends to secure.

5   Put the dough on a large baking sheet lined with baking paper. Cover with a lightly oiled piece of clingfilm and set aside in a warm place to prove for a further 35 minutes.

6   Preheat the oven to 220°C, fan 200°C, gas mark 7. Brush the dough with the beaten egg and bake for 35-40 minutes or until cooked through and golden. If the loaf is catching on top, cover loosely with foil. Allow to cool for 5 minutes, then slice and serve warm.

Garlic dough balls

makes 12   prep time 30 minutes + proving and cooling   cook time 15 minutes

3 3 3   87 kcal
per dough ball

Served warm from the oven, these tear-and-share soft rolls make a lovely accompaniment to a bowl of soup or a salad.

250g strong white bread flour, plus 10g for dusting

1 teaspoon caster sugar

½ teaspoon salt

1 teaspoon garlic granules

1.5g fast-action dried yeast

Calorie controlled cooking spray

1½ tablespoons low-fat spread

1 garlic clove, crushed

1 tablespoon finely chopped fresh flat-leaf parsley

1 Put the flour, sugar, salt and garlic granules into a large mixing bowl. Stir through the yeast and make a well in the centre. Pour 150ml warm water into the well and stir everything together to form a soft dough. Turn out onto a lightly floured surface and knead for 5-7 minutes or until smooth and springy.

2 Mist a large baking sheet with cooking spray. Divide the dough into 12 equal pieces, roll into balls and arrange them on the baking sheet, so they're almost touching. Cover with misted clingfilm and leave in a warm place for 35 minutes, or until doubled in size.

3 Preheat the oven to 220°C, fan 200°C, gas mark 7. In a small bowl, mash together the spread, garlic and parsley. Set aside.

4 Remove the clingfilm from the risen dough and bake for 15 minutes or until golden. Set aside to cool for 5 minutes, then brush with the garlic butter to serve, letting it melt over the dough balls.

Cook's tip
'Strong' flour has a higher gluten content than regular flour, giving a springier texture to bread dough.

Hot cross buns

makes 12 prep time 30 minutes + proving and cooling cook time 30 minutes

(8) (8) (8) 228 kcal per bun

If you like these classic Easter treats full of extra spice, boost the flavour even further with a pinch of ground cloves.

495g plain flour, plus 10g for dusting

1 teaspoon mixed spice

50g low-fat spread

7g sachet fast-action dried yeast

65g caster sugar

85g sultanas

40g currants

125ml skimmed milk, warmed

1 egg, lightly beaten

Calorie-controlled cooking spray

2 tablespoons low-calorie apricot jam, melted

Cook's tip

For chocolate hot cross buns, replace 10g of the flour in the dough with 10g cocoa powder, and omit the mixed spice. Replace the sultanas and currants with 100g milk chocolate chips.

(9) (9) (9)

1   Sift 450g flour and the mixed spice into a large mixing bowl and rub in the spread using your fingertips, until the mixture resembles fine breadcrumbs. Stir in the yeast, 55g sugar, sultanas and currants.

2   Whisk the milk, 80ml water and the egg together in a jug, using a fork. Make a well in the dry ingredients, pour in the wet ingredients and bring together as a sticky dough, using a wooden spoon.

3   Tip the dough onto a lightly floured surface and knead for 5-7 minutes until elastic. Return to the bowl, cover and leave to prove in a warm place for 1 hour or until doubled in size.

4   Preheat the oven to 200°C, fan 180°C, gas mark 6. Lightly mist an 18cm x 28cm baking tin with cooking spray. Knock back the dough with your fist to remove the excess air.

5   Divide the dough into 12 and roll into balls. Arrange in the prepared tin, cover again and set aside in a warm place for 30 minutes or until doubled in size. Make a flour paste by combining the remaining flour and sugar with about 2 tablespoons water in a small bowl. Transfer to a small food bag, snip off a corner and pipe crosses on the buns.

6   Bake for 10 minutes. Reduce the oven temperature to 180°C, fan 160°C, gas mark 4 and bake for a further 20 minutes until golden. Remove from the oven and set aside in the tin to cool slightly. Brush with the melted jam to glaze. Serve warm or at room temperature.

Seeded oat & rosemary loaf

serves 12   prep time 10 minutes + cooling   cook time 1 hour

3 **3** **1**   108 kcal
per serving

A chunky textured chewy loaf that goes well with soup when freshly baked, or can be toasted the next day.

Calorie controlled cooking spray

220g porridge oats

15g sunflower seeds

15g pumpkin seeds

1 teaspoon bicarbonate of soda

½ teaspoon salt

400g 0% fat natural Greek yogurt

1 egg, lightly beaten

½ tablespoon finely chopped fresh rosemary

1 Preheat the oven to 200°C, fan 180°C, gas mark 6. Mist a 900g loaf tin with cooking spray and line the base and sides with baking paper, leaving some overhang.

2 Blitz 70g of the porridge oats in a food processor until finely ground, then add to a large bowl along with all the remaining porridge oats. Add the rest of the ingredients, then stir until combined. Spoon the mixture into the prepared tin. Mist a sheet of foil with cooking spray and cover the tin, misted side down.

3 Bake for 30 minutes, then reduce the temperature to 180°C, fan 160°C, gas mark 4 and remove the foil. Continue to bake, uncovered, for 30 minutes or until golden and cooked through. Leave in the tin for 10 minutes to cool slightly then lift out. Cut into slices and serve warm.

Cook's tip
Use oats that are labelled as being gluten-free to make this a gluten-free loaf.

Soft pretzels

makes 12 **prep time 30 minutes** **cook time 15 minutes**

5 **5** **5** 175 kcal per pretzel

This typical American snack is surprisingly easy to make at home. Parboiling the shaped pretzels before baking gives them their characteristic chewy texture.

Calorie controlled cooking spray

540g gluten-free self-raising flour, plus 10g for dusting

7g sachet fast-action dried yeast

1 teaspoon table salt

1 tablespoon caster sugar

140g bicarbonate of soda, for boiling

2 teaspoons coarse or flaky sea salt

FOR THE MUSTARD DIP
4 tablespoons American-style mustard

1 tablespoon agave syrup

Cook's tip

Make your own 'everything bagel' seasoning, as an alternative topping to regular salt. Simply mix together ½ teaspoon each of sesame seeds, black sesame seeds and poppy seeds, ¼ teaspoon each of garlic granules and flaky sea salt plus 1 teaspoon crispy onion flakes.

6 **6** **6**

1. Preheat the oven to 220°C, fan 200°C, gas mark 7. Line 2 baking trays with baking paper; mist with cooking spray.

2. In a large bowl, combine the flour, yeast, salt and sugar, then gradually mix in 375ml warm water using a wooden spoon, until the mixture forms a smooth dough.

3. Put a large piece of baking paper on your work surface and dust with flour. Transfer the dough to the baking paper and shape into a ball. Press the ball into a circle then use a knife to divide the dough into 4 pieces. Cut each piece into 3 wedges. Mist all over with cooking spray to keep the dough from drying out while you shape the pretzels.

4. Roll each piece of dough into a smooth, 25cm-long rope. To form the pretzels, lay the rope in a horseshoe shape, with the open side towards you. Pick up the two ends and twist them around each other twice then take the tips back up to either side of the horseshoe shape. Press together gently, using a dab of water to secure if needed.

5. Put 3 litres water and the bicarbonate of soda in a large shallow pot and bring to a boil. Working in batches, use a large slotted spoon to add 2 or 3 pretzels to the pan (the water should be deep enough to cover them). Cook for 30 seconds, then lift out to the prepared trays. Repeat with the remaining pretzels. Scatter with the salt.

6. Bake for 10 minutes or until lightly browned and cooked through. Combine the mustard and agave syrup in a bowl for the dip; serve with the warm pretzels.

Mini plum turnovers

makes 12   **prep time 20 minutes + cooling**   **cook time 20 minutes**

4 **3** **3**   110 kcal
per turnover

Delicious served warm as a dessert or cold for teatime, these easy-to-make fruit-filled pastries are also great for taking on picnics.

250g plums, halved, stones removed and roughly chopped

1 star anise

1 cinnamon stick

1 tablespoon agave syrup

375g ready-rolled light puff pastry sheet (315g used)

1 egg, beaten

2 teaspoons icing sugar, to decorate

1   Put the plums in a pan with the star anise, cinnamon and agave syrup. Cover and cook over a low heat for 5 minutes, or until the plums start to soften. Remove the lid and continue to cook until the plums are sticky. Remove from the heat and set aside to cool, then remove and discard the star anise and cinnamon stick.

2   Preheat the oven to 200°C, fan 180°C, gas mark 6 and line a baking sheet with baking paper. Unroll the pastry on your work surface and cut into 12 x 8cm squares, discarding the trimmings. Put a spoonful of the spiced plum mixture on one corner of each square, then brush a little of the beaten egg around the edges. Fold over one corner to create a triangle and press with your fingers to seal the edges.

3   Put the turnovers on the prepared baking sheet and brush all over with the remaining egg. Bake for 15 minutes, or until crisp and golden. Leave to cool for 10 minutes, then serve dusted with the icing sugar.

Cook's tip

Change the flavour and replace the star anise and cinnamon with 8 cardamom pods, lightly crushed, plus 4 strips of orange zest, removed using a veg peeler.

Mini white chocolate & raspberry éclairs

makes 12   **prep time 20 minutes + cooling**   **cook time 15 minutes**

3 **2** **2**   67 kcal
per éclair

Filled with custard and raspberries and topped with pistachios and white chocolate, these petite éclairs make a pretty addition to any afternoon-tea table.

40g low-fat spread

50g plain flour, sifted

1 large egg, beaten

½ teaspoon powdered gelatine

100g low-fat ready-to-serve custard

55g fresh raspberries

50g white chocolate, broken into pieces

5g pistachio kernels, finely chopped

Cook's tip

Give these a 'Turkish delight' twist by stirring a couple of drops of rose water or orange flower water into the custard, after adding the gelatine.

1   Preheat the oven to 200°C, fan 180°C, gas mark 6. Line 2 baking trays with baking paper. Put the spread and 80ml cold water in a small pan. Bring to the boil, then remove from the heat and tip in the flour; beat with a wooden spoon for 1 minute, or until the mixture forms a smooth ball. Transfer to a heatproof bowl to cool slightly.

2   Using an electric hand-held whisk, beat in the egg, a little at a time, until the mixture is thick and glossy. Transfer the mixture to a piping bag fitted with a 1cm-round nozzle then pipe 12 x 7cm lengths, spaced at least 2.5cm apart, onto the lined trays. Bake for 15 minutes or until risen and golden. Turn off the oven and leave the éclairs to cool inside with the door closed, for 2 hours.

3   Put the gelatine in a heatproof jug with 1 tablespoon boiling water and stir until dissolved. Let cool for 5 minutes, then stir the mixture into the custard, cover with clingfilm and leave to reach room temperature. While the custard is cooling, put a few raspberries into the freezer. Crush the remaining raspberries and fold these into the custard.

4   Cut the éclairs in half lengthways and spoon 2 teaspoons of the custard mixture over each bottom half. Put the white chocolate into a microwave-safe bowl and melt in the microwave. Spread the melted chocolate over the éclair tops, then sandwich the halves together. Sprinkle over the chopped pistachios and crumble over the frozen raspberries to serve.

Apple pie

serves 6   prep time 30 minutes + cooling   cook time 55 minutes

8 **8** **8** 323 kcal per serving

A Sunday lunch classic, this comforting bake is made with an easy homemade dough crust and a puff pastry lid.

1kg eating apples, peeled, quartered, cored and cut into 1cm wedges

25g light brown soft sugar

1 tablespoon lemon juice

8g cornflour

Calorie controlled cooking spray

320g ready-rolled light puff pastry sheet (225g used)

110g plain flour, plus 5g for dusting

1 tablespoon icing sugar

¼ teaspoon bicarbonate of soda

¼ teaspoon salt

80g 0% fat natural Greek yogurt

1½ tablespoons skimmed milk

2 teaspoons demerara sugar

Cook's tip
Tossing the lightly cooked apples with cornflour avoids the risk of a 'soggy bottom' to the pie.

1 Preheat the oven to 200°C, fan 180°C, gas mark 6. Combine the apple, brown sugar and lemon juice in a pan set over a medium heat. Cook, covered, for 10 minutes or until the apple is just tender but still holds its shape. Remove from the heat, sprinkle over the cornflour and stir until well combined. Transfer the mixture to a large bowl and set aside to cool.

2 Lightly mist a 24cm (top measurement) pie tin with cooking spray. Unroll the pastry sheet on a baking tray lined with baking paper. Invert the pie tin onto the pastry and run a small knife around the edge to cut out a circle for the lid (if your pastry sheet isn't as wide as your pie tin, roll it out a little further first). Discard the trimmings. Cut out small leaf shapes from the pastry lid; lift them out and put them on the same tray. Chill until needed.

3 Sift the flour, icing sugar, bicarbonate of soda and salt into a bowl. Whisk the yogurt with 1 tablespoon of the milk in a small bowl. Stir the yogurt mixture into the flour mixture until it comes together. Knead the dough in the bowl for 2 minutes or until smooth. Roll out on a floured surface to make a 28cm round, then use to line the prepared tin, allowing it to overhang the edge slightly. Fill with the cooled apple mixture.

4 Cover with the puff pastry lid, pressing the edges to seal. Trim the edges, then decorate the rim of the pie lid with pastry leaves that you cut out earlier. Brush with the remaining milk and sprinkle over the demerara sugar. Bake for 40-45 minutes or until the pastry is puffed, golden and crisp. Serve warm, or at room temperature.

Spinach, walnut & feta rolls

makes 8   prep time 20 minutes + cooling   cook time 30 minutes

3 **3** **3**   107 kcal
per roll

A delicious vegetarian alternative to sausage rolls, these are just the thing
to take on a picnic or serve up for a light lunch.

**Calorie controlled
cooking spray**

1 large onion, finely chopped

200g young leaf spinach

100g light feta, crumbled

**25g walnut halves,
finely chopped**

40g fresh breadcrumbs

**2 x 45g sheets filo pastry
(25cm x 45cm)**

½ teaspoon sesame seeds

1 Mist a large frying pan with cooking spray and cook the
onion for 6-8 minutes over a medium heat until softened,
adding a splash of water if needed to stop it catching. Add
the spinach and cook until it has wilted and any moisture
has evaporated. Transfer to a plate and spread out to cool,
then squeeze out any excess liquid. Transfer to a bowl and
mix in the feta, walnuts and breadcrumbs, then season to
taste with pepper.

2 Preheat the oven to 220°C, fan 200°C, gas mark 7 and line
a baking sheet with baking paper. Mist the tops of both
sheets of filo with cooking spray, then lay one on top of
the other. Spoon the filling along one long side of the
pastry, then roll up like a sausage roll.

3 With the pastry seam underneath, make a few cuts
through the top of the filo to expose the filling, then slice
the roll into 8 equal pieces. Mist the tops with a little more
cooking spray and scatter over the sesame seeds. Put on
the prepared baking sheet and bake for 20 minutes or
until the pastry is crisp and golden, then serve.

Cook's tip
For an extra nutty flavour,
toast the walnuts on a tray
in the oven for 3-4 minutes
before chopping to use in
the filling.

Slow-roasted tomato tart

serves 6   prep time 20 minutes   cook time 1 hour 30 minutes

9 **9** **9**   269 kcal per serving

Using colourful mixed tomatoes makes this tart as pretty as a picture, but it tastes just as good made with regular tomatoes.

800g mixed tomatoes (we used golden cherry, baby plum and vine tomatoes), halved or quartered if large

1 teaspoon olive oil

1 tablespoon balsamic vinegar

Pinch of chilli flakes

375g ready-rolled light puff pastry sheet (340g used)

125g light mozzarella, very thinly sliced

Handful fresh basil leaves

1   Preheat the oven to 160°C, fan 140°C, gas mark 3. Put the tomatoes in a large roasting tin, drizzle over the oil and vinegar, then scatter over the chilli flakes. Season well and roast for 1 hour, until the tomatoes are starting to dehydrate. Remove from the oven and set aside.

2   Increase the oven temperature to 200°C, fan 180°C, gas mark 6 and line a baking sheet with baking paper. Unroll the pastry and trim the edges to a 20cm x 30cm rectangle, discarding the trimmings. Put the pastry on the prepared baking sheet and score a 1.5cm border. Prick the inner rectangle all over with a fork. Bake for 15 minutes, until the pastry has risen and is starting to turn golden.

3   Remove from the oven and arrange the tomatoes on the inner rectangle, leaving the border uncovered. Top the tomatoes with the mozzarella and return to the oven for another 10-12 minutes, or until the mozzarella is melted and golden. Remove from the oven and scatter over the basil leaves to serve.

Cook's tip

Boost the Mediterranean flavours by adding 1 red and 1 yellow pepper, deseeded and cut into eighths, to the tray of tomatoes to roast. The SmartPoints will stay the same.

Mushroom & Stilton free-form tarts

serves 6   **prep time 20 minutes**   **cook time 30 minutes**

(6) (6) (6)   214 kcal per tart   (symbol)

Ideal as a vegetarian main course for a special meal, these can be prepared a few hours ahead, ready to go in the oven when you are ready.

25g pine nuts

6 large flat mushrooms

6 small sage leaves

3 teaspoons olive oil

200g young leaf spinach

Small pinch ground nutmeg

6 x 45g sheets filo pastry (25cm x 45cm)

Calorie controlled cooking spray

35g Stilton, crumbled

Salad leaves, to serve

1 Preheat the oven to 190°C, fan 170°C, gas mark 5. Dry fry the pine nuts in a nonstick frying pan for 2-3 minutes until golden. Set aside.

2 Put the mushrooms, stalk-side up, on a large baking tray. Add a sage leaf plus ½ teaspoon oil and ½ teaspoon water to each mushroom and scatter on the pine nuts. Season then bake for 10-12 minutes, or until softened.

3 Meanwhile, wilt the spinach with 2 tablespoons water in a wok or large frying pan, stirring regularly. Season to taste with the nutmeg and some salt and pepper. Drain well then squeeze out any excess liquid. Chop and set aside.

4 To assemble the parcels, put one sheet of filo on a board and mist with cooking spray. Fold in half, then mist again. Put a spoonful of the chopped spinach in the centre, top with one of the mushrooms, then bring the corners of the pastry up and scrunch them loosely at the top to form a snug shell around the mushroom. Repeat with the remaining pastry, spinach and mushrooms, then scatter the Stilton between them. Transfer to 2 large baking trays and bake for 12-15 minutes, until the filo is crisp and golden. Serve immediately with salad.

Cook's tip
If you aren't keen on blue cheese, use the same quantity of feta instead, for the same SmartPoints.

Gypsy tart

serves 12   prep time 20 minutes + chilling and cooling   cook time 45 minutes

6 6 6   135 kcal
per serving

This Kentish treat is an old-fashioned favourite. The sweet fluffy filling is balanced by the tartness of crisp green apples.

160ml light evaporated milk

375g ready-rolled light shortcrust pastry sheet (275g used)

1 egg white, lightly whisked

100g dark brown soft sugar

1 green apple, cored and thinly sliced

Cook's tip
It's crucial that the evaporated milk is well chilled, or it won't whip up properly or be able to hold the volume when baked.

1 Before you start, make sure that the evaporated milk is very cold. Either put it in the fridge overnight, or in the freezer for a few hours until just starting to freeze.

2 Unroll the pastry and use it to line a 23cm round tart tin, trimming off the excess. Prick the base with a fork, then chill for 30 minutes. Preheat the oven to 190°C, fan 170°C, gas mark 5, with a baking tray on the centre shelf.

3 Line the pastry case with baking paper and add baking beans. Bake on the hot tray for 15 minutes until set. Remove the paper and beans then bake for a further 10 minutes until golden. Brush the tart case with the egg white to seal any cracks or holes. Allow to cool.

4 Add the chilled evaporated milk and sugar to the bowl of a stand mixer and whisk at a medium speed for 6-8 minutes until pale, soft and billowy, similar to meringue.

5 Spoon the mixture into the tart case and smooth with a spatula. Reduce the oven temperature to 150°C, fan 130°C, gas mark 2 and bake for 20 minutes until set on top but still a little wobbly – don't be tempted to over bake it, as this can cause the tart filling to collapse.

6 Remove from the oven and leave to cool completely, then chill to firm it up. Decorate the top of the tart with the apple slices just before serving.

Lemon meringue tartlets

makes 24   prep time 30 minutes + cooling   cook time 20 minutes

3 **3** **3**   76 kcal per tartlet

A pretty spin on a classic dessert that's ideal for elevenses – golden pastry shells filled with silky-smooth lemon curd and topped with crisp mini meringues.

375g ready-rolled light shortcrust pastry sheet (200g used)

3 lemons

20g cornflour

80g caster sugar

30g low-fat spread

2 egg yolks

24 x 5g mini meringues

YOU WILL ALSO NEED

24-hole mini pie tin

Cook's tip
You can freeze leftover egg whites – just make sure to label the container with the quantity. Use them for the Coffee meringue cake (page 54) .

1   Preheat the oven to 200°C, fan 180°C, gas mark 6. Unroll the pastry and use a 6cm round pastry cutter to stamp out 24 discs – you may need to re-roll the trimmings. Use the pastry to line a 24-hole mini pie tin (or 2 x 12-hole mini muffin tins).

2   Cut 24 small squares of baking paper and put a few baking beans in the middle of each piece. Scrunch the paper around the beans and put them in the pastry cases. Bake for 10-15 minutes, then remove the baking paper and beans and return to the oven to cook for a further 5 minutes, or until golden. Remove from the oven and leave to cool slightly in the tin, then transfer to a wire rack to cool completely.

3   Meanwhile, grate the zest from 2 of the lemons and squeeze the juice from all 3. Put the cornflour, lemon zest, lemon juice, and sugar in a pan with 4 tablespoons water. Heat over a gentle heat, stirring continuously, until the mixture comes to a boil and starts to thicken. Remove from the heat and whisk in the spread and egg yolks. Leave to cool slightly then spoon the curd mixture into the pastry tart cases and leave to cool completely.

4   Top each lemon tart with a mini meringue, then serve.

●   The tartlets will keep in an airtight container for up to 3 days.

Tiramisu roulade

serves 8   prep time 30 minutes + cooling   cook time 15 minutes

5 **4** **4**   103 kcal per serving

With all the flavours of the traditional Italian dessert, a light-as-a-feather chocolate sponge is rolled around a creamy coffee filling and finished with dark chocolate.

5 egg whites

¼ teaspoon cream of tartar

Pinch of salt

40g plain flour

2 tablespoons cocoa powder, plus an extra 1 teaspoon for dusting

100g caster sugar

1 tablespoon Marsala wine

10g dark chocolate, finely grated

FOR THE COFFEE CREAM FILLING

1 teaspoon instant coffee granules, dissolved in 1 teaspoon boiling water, cooled

½ tablespoon icing sugar

125g 0% fat quark

Cook's tip
You can replace the Marsala with 1 tablespoon of Irish cream liqueur.

5 **5** **5**

1 Preheat the oven to 180°C, fan 160°C, gas mark 4. Line a 20cm x 30cm swiss roll tin or baking tray with baking paper.

2 In a large mixing bowl, whisk the egg whites until foamy, then add the cream of tartar with a pinch of salt and continue to whisk until the mixture is stiff and forms peaks that hold their shape when the beaters are removed.

3 Sift the flour, 2 tablespoons cocoa and sugar over the egg white mixture, then gently fold until smooth and well combined.

4 Spoon the batter into the prepared tin and smooth the surface with a spatula. Bake for 12-15 minutes or until the sponge feels firm and springy to the touch.

5 Lightly dust a sheet of baking paper with 1 teaspoon cocoa powder. Turn the cake out onto the baking paper, peeling off and discarding the sheet from the tin, then roll up the roulade from one short side, with the cocoa-dusted paper inside as you roll. Set aside to cool.

6 To make the coffee cream filling, combine all the ingredients in a bowl, and mix until smooth and combined.

7 Unroll the sponge and drizzle or brush over the Marsala wine, then spread over the coffee cream filling. Scatter over half of the grated chocolate and re-roll the sponge, without the paper. Scatter the remaining chocolate over the top of the roulade and cut into slices to serve.

Baked vanilla cheesecake

serves 10   prep time 20 minutes + cooling   cook time 1 hour 5 minutes

(6) (6) (6)   175 kcal
per serving

Sun-ripened summer berries are the perfect contrast to the velvety texture
of this creamy baked cheesecake.

Calorie controlled
cooking spray

125g low-fat digestive biscuits

50g low-fat spread, melted

150g reduced-fat natural
cottage cheese

300g low-fat soft cheese

170g low-fat vanilla yogurt

3 eggs

1 teaspoon vanilla extract

40g caster sugar

125g strawberries, hulled
and halved

75g raspberries

75g blueberries

Cook's tip

Don't take a shortcut and
skip the step of sieving the
cottage cheese; it breaks
up the lumps far better
than a food processor can,
giving the cheesecake its
smooth texture.

1   Preheat the oven to 180°C, fan 160°C, gas mark 4. Mist a
18cm springform cake tin with cooking spray and line the
base with baking paper.

2   Put the biscuits in a food processor and blitz to a fine
crumb, or put them in a sealed plastic food bag and
crush with a rolling pin. Transfer to a mixing bowl and
stir in the melted spread until well combined. Press the
mixture evenly into the base of the prepared tin. Bake for
15 minutes, then remove from the oven and reduce the
temperature to 150°C, fan 130°C, gas mark 2.

3   Press the cottage cheese through a sieve and put into
a food processor. Add the soft cheese, yogurt, eggs,
vanilla extract and sugar and blitz until smooth. Pour
the mixture over the biscuit base and shake the tin
gently to level the surface.

4   Bake for 45-50 minutes until the cheesecake is set in the
centre but still slightly wobbly. Turn off the oven and
leave the cheesecake in the oven as it cools, for at least
1 hour – this gradual cooling helps stop the cheesecake
from cracking.

5   Chill until ready to serve, then carefully remove the
cheesecake from the tin and pile the berries on top – you
can serve any leftover berries on the side.

Chocolate & banana puddings

makes 4 **prep time 5 minutes + resting** **cook time 20 minutes**

4 **2** **2** 210 kcal
per pudding

Our take on melting-middle puddings is pretty close to wizardry: four key ingredients plus 5 minutes of prep is all that's needed for a pot of hot chocolate heaven.

Calorie controlled cooking spray

4 ripe bananas

4 eggs

4 tablespoons cocoa powder, plus ½ teaspoon for dusting

8 teaspoons low-calorie liquid chocolate shot

Cook's tip
For a salted caramel twist, use low-calorie caramel syrup instead of liquid chocolate shot in the pudding centres, adding a pinch of sea salt, for the same SmartPoints.

1   Preheat the oven to 180°C, fan 160°C, gas mark 4. Mist 4 ramekins or mini pudding basins with cooking spray and set aside.

2   Blend the bananas, eggs and cocoa powder in a food processor until smooth.

3   Spoon half the mixture into the ramekins or pudding basins, then add 2 teaspoons choc shot to each. Top with the remaining banana mixture and put on a baking tray. Bake for 15-20 minutes until risen and firm.

4   Remove from the oven, let stand for 2 minutes, then serve dusted with the extra cocoa powder.

Strawberry & pear bread puddings

makes 8   **prep time 15 minutes + soaking and resting**   **cook time 45 minutes**

5 **4** **4**   184 kcal per pudding

A fabulously fruity version of a family favourite recipe, baked individually to make them even more special.

Calorie controlled cooking spray

375ml skimmed milk

3 eggs

2 egg whites

1 teaspoon vanilla extract

8 x 35g slices white bread

100g low-calorie strawberry jam

2 x 415g tins pear halves in juice, drained, patted dry on kitchen paper and thickly sliced

250g strawberries, hulled and thickly sliced

1 teaspoon icing sugar, to decorate

1   Preheat the oven to 180°C, fan 160°C, gas mark 4. Mist 8 x 250ml ramekins or ovenproof dishes with cooking spray and place on a large baking tray.

2   Whisk the milk, eggs, egg whites and vanilla in a bowl until combined.

3   Spread one side of each slice of bread with the jam, then cut each into 8 small triangles. Arrange half the bread triangles, jam-side up and slightly overlapping, in the prepared dishes. Top with half of the pear and strawberry slices. Repeat with the remaining bread and fruit then pour over the egg mixture and set aside for 10 minutes for it to soak into the bread.

4   Bake for 45 minutes or until the puddings are set and golden; if the tops are browning too quickly, cover with a sheet of foil after about 30 minutes. Let stand for 20 minutes to cool slightly then serve warm or at room temperature, dusted with the icing sugar.

Cook's tip

You can bake this as one large pudding if you prefer, in which case cut the jammy slices of bread into quarters rather than eighths.

Recipe index

SmartPoints index

Green

1 SmartPoint
Strawberry 'meringue' drops — 18

2 SmartPoints
Cinnamon apple madeleines — 16
Mini lemon doughnuts — 24
Shortbread biscuits — 46

3 SmartPoints
Banana & date biscotti — 40
Chewy coconut cookies — 44
Chocolate muffins — 32
Garlic dough balls — 96
Lemon meringue tartlets — 118
Marshmallow squares — 64
Mini white chocolate éclairs — 106
Rocky road bites — 74
Seeded oat & rosemary loaf — 100
Spinach, walnut & feta rolls — 110
Victoria sponge bites — 26

4 SmartPoints
Chocolate & banana puddings — 124
Chocolate oaty digestives — 42
Fifteens — 14
Mini plum turnovers — 104
Pizza loaf — 94
Raspberry & coconut slice — 62
Ricotta cheese scones — 34
Soda bread — 92

5 SmartPoints
Apple & sultana cake — 78
Herby focaccia — 88
Pear & cranberry streusel bars — 70
Raspberry friands — 20
Soft pretzels — 102
Strawberry & pear bread puddings — 126
Tiramisu roulade — 120
Vegan choc chip cupcakes — 36

6 SmartPoints
Apple & maple syrup cupcakes — 38
Baked vanilla cheesecake — 122
Blackberry meringues — 22
Chocolate courgette brownies — 60
Cinnamon & pear cake — 52
Cinnamon rolls — 90
Gypsy tart — 116
Lamington traybake — 68
Mango, blueberry & lime traybake — 76
Marbled chocolate & banana loaf — 82
Mushroom & Stilton tarts — 114
Savoury breakfast muffins — 28
Strawberry Bakewell cake — 56
Sweet potato muffins — 30

7 SmartPoints
Blueberry yogurt cake — 80
Butternut squash cake — 84
Chocolate cake with sweet potato frosting — 66
Citrus upside-down cake — 58

8 SmartPoints
Apple pie — 108
Coffee meringue cake — 54
Forest fruit layer cake — 50
Hot cross buns — 98
Tottenham cake — 72

9 SmartPoints
Slow-roasted tomato tart — 112

Blue

1 SmartPoint
Chocolate muffins — 32
Strawberry 'meringue' drops — 18

2 SmartPoints
Chocolate & banana puddings — 124
Cinnamon apple madeleines — 16
Mini lemon doughnuts — 24
Mini white chocolate éclairs — 106
Shortbread biscuits — 46

3 SmartPoints
Banana & date biscotti — 40
Chewy coconut cookies — 44
Chocolate oaty digestives — 42
Garlic dough balls — 96
Lemon meringue tartlets — 118
Marshmallow squares — 64
Mini plum turnovers — 104
Rocky road bites — 74
Seeded oat & rosemary loaf — 100
Spinach, walnut & feta rolls — 110
Victoria sponge bites — 26

4 SmartPoints
Apple & sultana cake — 78
Fifteens — 14
Pizza loaf — 94
Raspberry & coconut slice — 62
Ricotta cheese scones — 34
Soda bread — 92
Strawberry & pear bread puddings — 126
Tiramisu roulade — 120

5 SmartPoints
Cinnamon rolls — 90
Herby focaccia — 88
Mango, blueberry & lime traybake — 76
Pear & cranberry streusel bars — 70
Raspberry friands — 20
Savoury breakfast muffins — 28
Soft pretzels — 102
Strawberry Bakewell cake — 56
Sweet potato muffins — 30
Vegan choc chip cupcakes — 36

6 SmartPoints
Apple & maple syrup cupcakes — 38
Baked vanilla cheesecake — 122
Blackberry meringues — 22
Blueberry yogurt cake — 80
Chocolate courgette brownies — 60
Cinnamon & pear cake — 52
Citrus upside-down cake — 58
Forest fruit layer cake — 50
Gypsy tart — 116
Lamington traybake — 68
Marbled chocolate & banana loaf — 82
Mushroom & Stilton tarts — 114

7 SmartPoints
Butternut squash cake — 84
Chocolate cake with sweet potato frosting — 66

8 SmartPoints
Apple pie — 108
Coffee meringue cake — 54
Hot cross buns — 98
Tottenham cake — 72

9 SmartPoints
Slow-roasted tomato tart — 112

Purple

1 SmartPoint
Chocolate muffins — 32
Seeded oat & rosemary loaf — 100
Strawberry 'meringue' drops — 18

2 SmartPoints
Chocolate & banana puddings — 124
Cinnamon apple madeleines — 16
Mini lemon doughnuts — 24
Mini white chocolate éclairs — 106
Shortbread biscuits — 46

3 SmartPoints
Banana & date biscotti — 40
Chewy coconut cookies — 44
Chocolate oaty digestives — 42
Garlic dough balls — 96
Lemon meringue tartlets — 118
Marshmallow squares — 64
Mini plum turnovers — 104
Rocky road bites — 74
Soda bread — 92
Spinach, walnut & feta rolls — 110
Victoria sponge bites — 26

4 SmartPoints
Apple & sultana cake — 78
Fifteens — 14
Mango, blueberry & lime traybake — 76
Pear & cranberry streusel bars — 70
Pizza loaf — 94
Raspberry & coconut slice — 62
Ricotta cheese scones — 34
Strawberry & pear bread puddings — 126
Tiramisu roulade — 120

5 SmartPoints
Cinnamon rolls — 90
Herby focaccia — 88
Raspberry friands — 20
Savoury breakfast muffins — 28
Soft pretzels — 102
Strawberry Bakewell cake — 56
Sweet potato muffins — 30
Vegan choc chip cupcakes — 36

6 SmartPoints
Apple & maple syrup cupcakes — 38
Baked vanilla cheesecake — 122
Blackberry meringues — 22
Blueberry yogurt cake — 80
Chocolate cake with sweet potato frosting — 66
Chocolate courgette brownies — 60
Cinnamon & pear cake — 52
Citrus upside-down cake — 58
Forest fruit layer cake — 50
Gypsy tart — 116
Lamington traybake — 68
Marbled chocolate & banana loaf — 82
Mushroom & Stilton tarts — 114

7 SmartPoints
Butternut squash cake — 84

8 SmartPoints
Apple pie — 108
Coffee meringue cake — 54
Hot cross buns — 98
Tottenham cake — 72

9 SmartPoints
Slow-roasted tomato tart — 112